We're Still Here:
Contemporary Virginia Indians Tell Their Stories

We're Still Here:
Contemporary Virginia Indians
Tell Their Stories

Sandra F. Waugaman and
Danielle Moretti-Langholtz, Ph.D.

palari
Publishing

Richmond, Virginia

We're Still Here: Contemporary Virginia Indians Tell Their Stories
©2000, 2001, 2006 by Sandra F. Waugaman & Danielle Moretti-Langholtz
Second Printing 2001, revised
Third Printing 2006, revised

Published by Palari Publishing
WWW.PALARIBOOKS.COM

Library of Congress Catalog Card Number: 00-102427

ISBN 13: 9781928662013
ISBN 10: 1928662013
Printed in the United States of America

Cover: Troy L. Adkins, Chickahominy Indian and former
member of the Virginia Council on Indians.
Title Page: Preston Adkins, Chickahominy Indian
and traditional dancer.

Photos: All photographs, except where otherwise
noted, are by Sandra F. Waugaman.

Prints: Theodore DeBry engravings courtesy of
American Indian History and Related issues at
www.csulb.edu/projects/ais/

Contents

Foreword

This book would not have been possible without the cooperation of the many Virginia Indians who so patiently and generously gave of their time and knowledge in interviews with the authors. The authors want to give special thanks to these past and present chiefs of the state-recognized tribes in Virginia:

- Leonard Adkins, Chickahominy Tribe
- Marvin Bradby, Eastern Chickahominy Tribe
- Webster Custalow, Mattaponi Tribe
- Kenneth Branham, Monacan Nation
- Barry W. Bass, Nansemond Tribe
- William Miles, Pamunkey Tribe
- G. Anne Richardson, Rappahannock Tribe
- Edmund Adams, Upper Mattaponi Tribe

We would also like to thank:
- Chief Emeritus Oliver Perry, Nansemond Tribe
- Dr. Linwood Custalow, Mattaponi Tribe
- Chief Robert Green, Patawomeck Tribe.

Their support is greatly appreciated.

We would also like to thank Margaret C. Cook, Curator of Rare Books and Manuscripts at the

Swem Library, for her assistance in obtaining the John Smith map.

Thanks also to Elizabeth Hedgepeth of the *Petersburg Progress-Index,* and David Fritz of Staunton's *Daily News Leader.*

Each author brought unique talents to the project—Sandra Waugaman as an award-winning writer and photographer, and Professor Danielle Moretti-Langholtz as a cultural anthropologist.

Sandra was assigned to write a magazine article about Indians living in the Richmond area for *Richmond Magazine* in 1997. At that time she knew very little about the subject. She was put in contact with Mary Wade, a Monacan Indian, then serving as secretary of the Virginia Council on Indians. Mary introduced Sandra to many knowledgeable Indians who patiently answered countless questions. Reeva Tilley, a Rappahannock Indian, and Nita Smith, a Nansemond, were particularly helpful; and also introduced Sandra to other members of their families and tribes.

Soon Sandra began visiting some of the historical sites in Virginia, and writing articles about Indian museums and the two reservations. As Sandra interviewed more and more Indians she realized that each interview usually ended the same way, with the individual saying, "Just tell people we're still here." It seemed that request could best be answered by a book.

After hearing Danielle speak at the 1998 Governor's Conference on Indian Affairs, Sandra approached her with the idea of gaining support for such a book. Danielle also felt there was a need for a book on contemporary Virginia Indians, and offered to join in the endeavor.

In her anthropological work, Danielle has focused on the resurgence of American Indians during the twentieth century, and has been involved in a number of wide-ranging projects with tribes from several regions of the United States. She has worked at the Oklahoma Museum of Natural History in Norman, Oklahoma, and the American Museum of Natural History in New York City, in both collections management and issues pertaining to repatriation. After relocating to Virginia and teaching at the College of William & Mary, Danielle had the good fortune to meet and work closely with the late Thomasina Jordan, Chair of the Virginia Council on Indians. This involvement introduced Danielle to the concerns of the Virginia Indian population, foremost among these the need to address issues of their identity and history in their own voices.

One book cannot possibly present all there is to know about Virginia's Indians. There are many complicated issues that are merely introduced here. But hopefully this book will dispel some of the popular stereotypes, while introducing readers to some interesting people who also happen to be Indians. The authors feel honored that so many were willing to share their unique stories. This book provides an insight into the history, education, and cultural traditions of each state-recognized tribe in Virginia. Through personal accounts of Indians in Virginia, the reader will become familiar with the hardships Virginia Indians have had to endure, and how they continue to struggle for the recognition they deserve.

Prologue

Indelible Thread of Red

The late Thomasina Jordan, the first American Indian chair of the Virginia Council on Indians, often said to look for the "indelible thread of red" in the tapestry of the American people. She believed strongly that the thread of red, which to her symbolized the history, culture and importance of American Indians in our national heritage, could never be eliminated. Thomasina's beautiful metaphor is a reminder to all of us that we should seek out the "thread of red" and thereby enrich our own understanding of the place of American Indians in the history of our nation and state.

Thomasina Jordan, the first American Indian chair of the Virginia Council on Indians.

While people are genuinely interested in learning about American Indians, they often overlook Virginia's indigenous people. We found that frequently people ask, "Are there any Indians left in Virginia?" Conversely, Virginia Indians ask, "Why don't people know we're still here?" It is clear that the two questions are linked, and point to a major omission in the construction and recounting of our history. Indeed, Chief Barry Bass, of the Nansemond Tribe, feels that "educating the general public that Virginia Indians still exist" is one of the single most important issues facing the tribes today. "First and foremost, the public needs to know something about the

Educating the general public that Virginia Indians still exist is one of the single most important issues facing the tribes today.

1

true history of the Indian people. We do not feel that our history has been told accurately or fully."

For too long the legacy of Virginia's Indian population has been both understudied and narrowly focused on the first half of the 16th century. The epic figures of Chief Powhatan and his famous daughter Pocahontas stand alongside the equally famous John Smith and John Rolfe in the distant haze of the historical past. The critical role that Virginia Indians played in the initial years of the European colonization of North America is dutifully noted in both our national and state historical text. However, the Indians of Virginia are rarely mentioned in the post-17th century accounts of the Commonwealth of Virginia. Virginia Indians practically disappear from the pages of both America's and Virginia's history by the time the 18th century is discussed in textbooks. This invisibility has led most people to falsely conclude that Virginia's Indian population must have vanished long ago.

Virginia Indians Today — In 2000 approximately 21,000 American Indians resided in the Commonwealth of Virginia. Most are not indigenous, or native, to Virginia but are the descendants of many different Indian tribes who, for various reasons, choose to live in the Commonwealth. The complex whole that represents Virginia's Native American population has its roots in the more than 500 diverse American Indian cultures and historical traditions that once dominated all of the North American continent. However, this book is concerned with the story of Virginia Indians, the descendants of those tribes indigenous to the Commonwealth in 1607.

Authentic, contemporary Virginia tribes —Virginia's modern indigenous community takes its

Statue of Pocahontas by Adolf Sehring located in Gloucester, VA.

2

form from the past. The threads of the tapestry of Virginia Indian identity link the contemporary tribes with the ancestral tribes known to us from the 17th century. As is true throughout the United States, in the Commonwealth of Virginia a standard of proof has been devised to validate and officially "recognize" Indian tribes. The Virginia Council on Indians, a state-sponsored advisory committee established in 1983, has adopted criteria to help clarify issues of Virginia Indian tribal identity. According to the Virginia Council on Indians, legitimate and recognized Virginia tribes are "those indigenous tribes which were living on a site in what is now the Commonwealth of Virginia at the time of the arrival of the first European settlers. The current members of those tribes are Indian descendants of those indigenous tribes with appropriate records and historical documentation." Thus, Virginia Indian identity is grounded in an historical experience as well as the contemporary Virginia Indian community, a network of personal relationships and the intact political organization of the modern tribe. It is a complex and venerable tapestry indeed.

Documenting the past — Historians have relied on documents and maps written by Europeans during the early "Contact" Period and the initial years of settlement to reconstruct the indigenous Indian world. Anthropologists have relied on archaeological excavations and interviews with contemporary Virginia Indians to reconstruct the "pre-Contact" and "post-Contact" culture of our first inhabitants. Nevertheless, it is difficult to identify with certainty the exact number and the specific names of the tribes that lived in Virginia in the early 17th century. Since the documents were written by the newcomers to Virginia these people were not familiar with the region or native languages. We cannot be sure the English understood the nature of the relationship among the various tribes or even wrote down their correct tribal names. Moreover, the turmoil that followed the establishment of the Jamestown settlement permanently altered the political and cultural landscape of Virginia's Indian population, thus further complicating our ability to understand the complexities of pre-contact indigenous society.

American Indian tribal cultures — For thousands of years the entire North American continent was the domain of a people whose lifeways and languages were diverse beyond imagination. The "First Americans" subsisted by developing strategies for utilizing the resources in their environments. Some groups were horticulturalists and some fished, hunted, and gathered edible plants, seeds and nuts as the seasons allowed. They were well-adapted to their local environments and by following an annual cycle of hunting, fishing, gathering and planting avoided putting pressure on any single food resource. We know that the Powhatans called their beautiful Virginia homeland *Tsenacommacah*. They lived in sedentary villages and hunted, fished, gathered, and cultivated gardens of corn, beans and squash.

Virginia's Indian population after colonization — During the 1600s, interactions between the European settlers and the indigenous population brought tremendous change to the culture, politics and religious life of Virginia's indigenous tribes. The impact of European diseases was devastating to native populations throughout North and South America. The ensuing decades of cross-cultural conflict led to a period of demographic collapse for Vir-

TRIBAL CULTURES

ginia Indians. Periods of starvation and the successive surrender of large areas of land to the colonists brought irreversible changes to the Indian world. The majority of Virginia's indigenous tribes were destroyed in the colonial experience and no longer exist. This is one of the saddest legacies of the colonial encounter.

In the trauma of the post-colonial world, Powhatans and other Virginia tribes were forced to implement drastic survival strategies. Those few Indians who survived the fighting, onslaught of diseases, enslavement, and attempts at cultural destruction sought to sustain themselves by fishing, hunting and continuing their agricultural practices as far away from the English settlements as possible. In time even these relatively remote pockets of Indian habitation were surrounded by non-Indian settlers, further threatening the existence of the remaining Virginia Indian population.

In 1677, with the signing of the Treaty of Middle Plantation, the insatiable appetite for land on the part of the English settlers resulted in the establishment of a number of Indian reservations in the colony of Virginia. The treaty also forced the Indians living on reservations to pay annual taxes (or tribute) to the Governor (which they have continued to do without interruption), and to submit to numerous harsh measures imposed by the British Crown. During the 18th century, Virginia Indians gradually lost control of their reservations, and with this near total land loss vestigial elements of Indian political sovereignty were nearly lost as well.

Virginia tribal heritage — Despite the enormous pressure on Indians to cede their traditional homelands to the colonizers, attempts to destroy the traditional cultural practices of our first

The Treaty of Middle Plantation was signed in 1677.

5

inhabitants, and the enactment of legislation designed to deny their existence, American Indians have survived in Virginia to the present day. Eight Virginia tribes can trace their heritage back to the period of European contact and using archaeological evidence, even further back in time. In an extraordinary demonstration of tenacity and survival, the Mattaponi and Pamunkey tribes have held on to their original 16th-century reservations, making them two of the oldest extant reservations in the United States.

The Mattaponi and Pamunkey Tribes have played an important role in the political and cultural revitalization of Virginia's other Indian tribes. Living along the rivers of their namesakes, the Mattaponi and Pamunkey people have continued some of the traditional subsistence practices of their ancestors. Avid fishermen, members of both tribes participate in shad fishing and maintain fish hatcheries that have done much to keep the shad population viable in Virginia.

The 20th century was a time of both tragedy and triumph for Virginia's Indians. That century bore witness to repressive legislation—the Racial Integrity Act of 1924, which attempted to deny the existence of the surviving Indian population in the Commonwealth. After more than three centuries of relentless pressure on native communities, Virginia attempted to legislate the remnants of Virginia's First Nations out of existence. This harsh and restrictive legislation was not repealed until 1968. However, with desegregation and the changing racial climate in Virginia, the Indian community became stronger and reemerged with a more public presence in the state and the nation.

In 1983, the General Assembly of the Commonwealth of Virginia granted formal state recogni-

6

tion to six of Virginia's indigenous tribes in House Joint Resolution No. 54. Along with the reserved tribes—the Mattaponi and Pamunkey—the Commonwealth recognized the Chickahominy, the Eastern Division of the Chickahominy, the Upper Mattaponi, and the Rappahannock Tribes. In 1985 the Nansemond Tribe was granted state recognition with the passage of House Joint Resolution No. 205, and the Monacan Tribe achieved state recognition in 1989 under House Joint Resolution No. 390. All of the foregoing tribes except the Monacan Nation were associated with the Powhatan Chiefdom.

The 21st century began on a sad note with the passing of Chief Leonard Adkins on March 10, 2001. He served the Chickahominy Tribe for 51 years being elected assistant chief in 1951, and then chief in 1986, a position he held until his death on March 10, 2001.

He grew up in a time when educational opportunities were not open to Indian people beyond the 7th grade in Virginia, so after completing the 7th grade, he worked on the family farm until he was old enough to enter the military. After completing his service to his country, he returned home

to finish the 8th grade, which had been added to the school during his absence. He went to Oklahoma where he finished his high school education, and earned a two-year associate degree from Bacone

Chief Leonard Adkins of the Chickahominy Tribe.

7

Indian School. When he returned to the Chickahominy community, he taught at the Samaria Indian
School. He taught for 35 years in various schools
both before and after desegregation, receiving
bachelors and masters degrees in Elementary Education from Virginia Commonwealth University
along the way.

Even after his retirement he continued to
work with young people, encouraging them to further
their education. He was looking forward to a future
when the Chickahominy, as well as other state recognized tribes, would receive federal recognition.

The future of Virginia Indians — Kenneth
Branham, Chief of the Monacan Indian Nation,
speaking about the future of his tribe, says, "This is a
new chapter in the history of Virginia Indians. We are
reclaiming our history. For example, our people are
committed to building an authentic replica of a
Monacan village in partnership with Natural Bridge
Park. It will be an educational experience for visitors
to the Natural Bridge to learn about the everyday
Monacan life of 400 years ago. But it will also be an
opportunity to teach our own people our traditional
ways. I've never seen this much excitement in
the tribe."

Indeed, the indelible thread of red is more
visible in the rich tapestry of the American people
than it has been for many years. The voices of Virginia Indian people have grown proud and strong
once again and this is our opportunity to listen to
what they have to say.

Chapter 1

The Pamunkey and Mattaponi: Living on the Reservation

Misconceptions are a daily challenge to Virginia Indians. "You can see it in their eyes," says Bill Miles, chief of the Pamunkey Indians. "When people visit our reservation they look all around. They're looking for the tepees." He adds, "Well, the Pamunkey never did live in tepees, not even in the 17th century. They lived in long-houses and today we live just like everyone else."

A model of a yehakin at Jamestown in the recreated Powhatan Indian Village.

Yehakins are large one-room shelters made of dried grass mats sewn together over bent, tied saplings.

The houses on the reservation in King William County do look like houses in any rural community in Virginia. There are TV antennas, a satellite dish here and there, wash hanging on clotheslines, and small trucks and SUVs parked in the driveways. But this is not any rural community in Virginia. The Paumunkey and the Mattaponi Reservations, just a few miles away, are two of the oldest Indian reservations in the United States.

Once you cross into the reservations you leave Virginia and enter a state within a state. Chief Miles says, "The reservations were established as sovereign states by treaty with the British Government, before there was a United States. We deal with state and local governments on a state-to-state basis."

We're Still Here

Treaties:

1646 —
Prevented Indians
from entering English
settlements.

1650 —
Reserved land for
Indian towns.

1677 —
Acknowledged
Indian leaders' sub-
jection to King of
England and estab-
lished the six reser-
vations.

There were several treaties with the British; some restricted the Indians' movements, others established reservations. A 1646 treaty prevented Indians from entering English settlements. The only ones allowed onto the land controlled by the English were messengers sent by the chiefs, and they had to wear striped coats to identify themselves. Eventually the striped coats were replaced with badges inscribed with the name of their chief. In this same year, it became an offense punishable by death to entertain or conceal Indians within the bounds of English-controlled territory.

In 1650 another treaty reserved land for Indian towns, allowing 50 acres per warrior. In following years other laws were passed, and the land reserved for the Indians grew smaller and smaller.

In May of 1677 a treaty was signed by many Indian leaders at Middle Plantation. By signing this treaty the Indian leaders acknowledged their subjection to the King of England and they agreed to "pay their Tribute to the Right hon'ble his Ma'ties Govern'r for the time being." Article seven of this treaty ensured "That the said Indians have and enjoy theire wonted conveniences of Oystering, fishing, and gathering Tuccahoe, Curttennemmons, wild oats, rushes, Puckoone, or any thing else for their natural Support not usefull to the English, upon the English Devidends." It also stated that before they entered those areas they had to inform a public magestrate of their intentions, receive a certificate, and then go directly home "without wearing or carrying any manner of weapon, or lodging under any Englishman's dwelling house on night."

This treaty also established six reservations. Gradually, for a variety of reasons, most of the tribes

The Pamunkey and Mattaponi: Living on the Reservation

lost their reservations.

By 1748, the Pamunkey and the Mattaponi were the only tribes that still lived on the land held in trust for them by what had become the state of Virginia. They never owned the land under the trust agreement; therefore, they never had to pay state, property, or real estate taxes. The Indians continued to adhere to the terms of the 1677 treaty, and after the Revolutionary War that tribute was (and still is) paid to the governor of Virginia.

The Mattaponi and Pamunkey reservations are governed by an elected chief, one or more assistant chiefs, and a tribal council.

The chief of the Pamunkey, William "Swift Water" Miles, was not born on the reservation. It has never been easy to make a living in a rural county like King William, and during the depression it became almost impossible. In hopes of finding a better economic situation in the North, the Miles family moved to New Jersey. His father returned in 1976, was elected chief in 1984, and served as chief until 1990. Chief Miles returned to the reservation in

Governor Mark Warner accepting the ceremonial payment of taxes.

Webster "Little Eagle" Custalow, Chief, Mattaponi Tribe (2001).

William "Swift Water" Miles, Chief, Pamunkey Tribe (2000).

We're Still Here

Michaele White, courtesy Governor's Office

Governor and Mrs. Gilmore at the ceremonial payment of taxes (November 1999).

1982 and was elected chief in 1990.

One of the duties of the chief of the reservated tribes is to make the tribute presentation to the governor. Originally the treaty specified that the Indians present three arrows and twenty beaver pelts. In the past few years the arrows and pelts have been replaced with an offering of game, usually a deer, and pottery or a "peace pipe." Once scheduled for March, the ceremony now takes place the day before Thanksgiving.

It has always been important to the Indians to adhere to the conditions for the tribute set forth in the treaty, and sometimes they have had to go to extreme measures to meet those conditions.

Chief Miles remembers one year when it was particularly difficult to obtain the game for the tribute. "We always have a big hunt the week before Thanksgiving. Members of the tribe who do not live on the reservation come back, and we hunt turkey and deer. Usually we get enough to give the governor a nice deer, and have enough game for others to eat during the winter. But one year, we couldn't find anything, no deer, no turkeys—nothing. My dad was chief then, and he knew we had to have something to present to the governor; so he went to a turkey farm, bought a live turkey, brought it back to the reservation and killed it. That way we were able to fulfill the terms of the treaty—after all it was killed on the reservation."

People often think that Indians living on a reservation do not pay any federal or state taxes. Carl "Lone Eagle" Custalow, chief of the Mattaponi, says, "The only taxes we do not pay are property taxes and income taxes on anything we produce on the reservation. If we catch fish from the Mattaponi River and sell them, we don't pay taxes on that money. But I work away from the reservation, so I pay the same income taxes as everyone else. And there is a catch to not paying property taxes. When you live on the reservation you don't actually own the land your house is on. The land is held in trust for the tribe by the State of Virginia. So when you go to get financing to build a house, it's difficult because you don't have the deed to the property. That's why I built my house myself. It took me ten years, but I finally did it."

Chief Custalow was born at his parent's home on the Mattaponi Reservation along with his eight brothers and sisters. He remembers that his family worked hard just to survive. "Our only means of income was farming or the river. Everyone had their own garden, and a cow for milk and butter. We hunted different animals, and raised our own hogs. Each house had a garden plot, and we grew vegetables that were canned for the winter. Back then we didn't have as many houses on the reservation, but we had a lot of kids. And the kids all worked in the gardens, and had their chores. Everyone worked in

FISHING

MATTAPONI RIVER

harmony; the whole family worked together. It was not girls doing this or boys doing that. The girls fished and did their chores just like the boys."

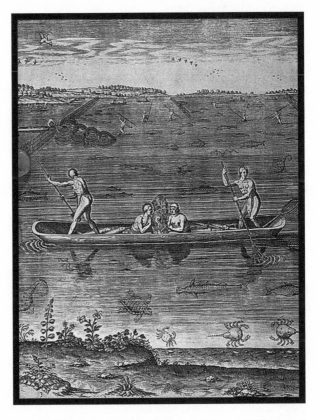

Weir is a trap set in a stream or waterway for catching fish.

Fishing on the Mattaponi and Pamunkey Rivers is part of the Indians' traditional heritage. From the very beginning the early settlers wrote about the methods they observed. They recorded that Indians used traps (or weirs) and nets. In addition, a 16th-century engraving by Theodore DeBry (above) showed Indians fishing at night, burning fires in their boats to attract the fish which they then speared.

Some of the old methods continue to be used, and some of the earliest memories Assistant Chief Custalow has are of fishing. His father taught him to fish, and most children on the reservation learned to fish. Now, in the 21st century, the Indians are still fishing with gill nets during the shad and herring runs in the spring.

The Mattaponi is a tidal river. Four tides make a day, with high water every seven hours and low every five. People usually fish all four tides. Chief Custalow explains, "When I was young the nets were made out of cotton, and the fish would make knots in the nets trying to get out. We called them tangles, and they had to be cleared before you could fish the next tide. As a kid we were always glad to see shad season over, because we could be sound asleep, and Daddy would come home at 1:00 a.m. and wake us up to clear his nets. He had to get some sleep before the next tide, but we had to get up and go to school the next morning. And if there were nine kids, nine kids got up and cleared those nets."

As a child it just seemed like hard work, but looking back he remembers that it was also a beautiful sight. Although they did not use fires to attract the fish, there were still fires on the river. The fish started to run when it was still pretty cold, especially at night. "Sometimes we built a fire in the boat to stay warm. Now that I think about it, I guess it was dangerous because we took a can of kerosene, put a rag in it, and lit it. We also built fires on the shore. If a net got messed up, we had to come in to shore to untangle the net, and we needed the fire for light. We also used lanterns to keep track of the nets. Because it was a tidal river a net might drift off, so we made a lantern board and put a lantern on it and tied that onto each end of the net. When I was a kid you could walk down here at night and it looked like a little city with the lights out there. It was a sight to see. There were ten or twelve fishermen, and each one had four or five nets so there were lots of lights. It was a beautiful sight."

Chief Custalow still fishes, but not with cotton nets. Nylon nets replaced the cotton, and now the nets are made out of monofiliment, which doesn't tangle. He still uses some of the nylon nets in addition to his two monofiliment nets. He continues to attach a lantern to each net at night to see where it is, but now he only uses one lantern per net.

Indians have always believed that you can't just take from the land, you have to give back for future generations. When commercial fishermen catch a spawning shad, they sell it—eggs and all. But the Indians use those eggs to help new fish hatch. To do this, the Mattaponi built a shad hatchery on the Mattaponi River in 1916, and the Pamunkey built one on the Pamunkey River in 1918.

Chief Miles explained that when the shad are caught fishermen take a female fish and run their hands down the belly to milk the eggs into a bucket of river water they have in their boat. Then they take a buck shad and milk the sperm out of him into the same bucket. He said, "When the boats come in to shore, the buckets are emptied into special tanks. You can actually watch the eggs swell up. It takes about three to five days for the eggs to hatch out, and then they look like little dots. For 21 days they are fed brine shrimp, and then they are flushed out into the river. There are fifteen tanks. In the center of each tank is a tube connected to a pipe that leads to the river. When the time is right, the tube is pulled up and everything goes out into the river. It's just like pulling up a stopper in a bathtub. Last year we got a grant from the Chesapeake Bay Program to expand our hatchery from three holding tanks to fifteen."

SHAD HATCHERY

The Pamunkey and Mattaponi: Living on the Reservation

Chief Miles estimates that in 1998 they put seven million fry back into the river, and in 1999 that probably tripled.

At one time both reservations had their own schools. The agreement was that if the Indians built a school the State of Virginia would supply books, a teacher and food for lunch to each reservation. By 1955 there were not enough children at the Pamunkey Reservation to justify a school. It was closed, and the Pamunkey children were bused to the one-room school on the Mattaponi Reservation. As desegregation was implemented in Virginia in the 1960s, the Mattaponi school was closed too, and the children began to attend the King William County Public Schools.

Chief Custalow remembers going to the Mattaponi school. "They had one teacher for the first eight grades, and one teacher for grades nine through twelve. We really didn't learn a lot. The teacher didn't have much time to teach. About all she had time to do was give you homework and take up papers." He left the reservation to attend high school

Hatchery tanks in the Pamunkey Fish Hatchery on the Pamunkey Reservation.

(inset): John H. Langston opens valve to let shad fry move into a tank (2001).

EDUCATION

in Richmond, and eventually graduated from the University of Richmond.

Although he understands the teachers were not properly educated about Indians, Custalow can't help expressing his resentment about one particular incident. "In the fourth grade we learned about Virginia history. And our teacher told us about the colonists and Indians, and that the Indians were all savages. Here we were, in our own school, on our own reservation, being taught we were savages. At the time it didn't dawn on us what was going on, but now I'd like to turn back time and teach history right. Those history books were written from one perspective, and by repeating what was written down by people who were our enemies. They called themselves superior. But we were the ones who taught them how to survive in the land, and we learned their language — they couldn't learn ours."

Chapter 2

Remembering the Past

Today, Indians attempt to correct stereotypes that are centuries old. "We were not savages, barbarians, nor heathens." Oliver Perry, Chief Emeritus of the Nansemond tribe stated emphatically. The problem is "what was written in the history books was slanted and written from the viewpoint of the so-called 'conquerors'. I was familiar with the oral history that was passed down from my mother and her sisters. I remember going to the home of the late Chief Earl Bass when I was young and hearing stories about relatives and all." Chief Emeritus Perry's memory of family stories aided the formal reorganization of the Nansemond Tribe.

In 1985, he was instrumental in compiling the

(left to right)
Chief Barry Bass,
Nansemond Tribe;
Chief G. Anne
Richardson,
Rappahannock Tribe;
and Chief Arthur L.
Adkins,
Chickahominy Tribe
(2000).

TRIBAL RECOGNITION

documentation on the Nansemond tribe. "What cemented it all was the desire of certain individuals to get formal recognition for the tribe. After 1983 when six Virginia tribes were recognized by the General Assembly, we began to ask why the Nansemonds didn't get included in the legislation. We knew that we were a legitimate tribe, but we had been functioning informally because of the stress related to racial laws in the Commonwealth since the 18th century. I decided to search for documents to substantiate what I had been told about the Nansemonds since I was a child so that our tribe could also obtain formal recognition."

Chief Emeritus Perry spent several years in search of documentation that would give formal recognition to the Nansemond Tribe, one of the historical tribes of the Powhatan chieftaincy. At the time of English settlement, the chiefdom was under the control of a formidable political leader whose personal name was Wahunsunacock, but was known publicly as Powhatan. The chiefdom was composed of 30 or more tribes from as far north as the Potomac River, as far south as Chesapeake, Virginia, and parts of the Eastern Shore. Seven of the eight state-recognized tribes were part of the Powhatan chiefdom. They are the Chickahominy, Eastern Division Chickahominy, Mattaponi, Upper Mattaponi, Nansemond, Pamunkey, and Rappahannock. The Patawomecks and the Accohannocks, also former members of the Powhatan chiefdom, are organized tribes, but they do not have state recognition.

> Seven of the eight state-recognized tribes were part of the Powhatan chiefdom.

LANGUAGE

The Powhatans were Algonquian-speaking Indians. Algonquian-speaking tribes lived along the Northeast coast of the United States, along the St. Lawrence River and as far west as the Great Lakes. They may have shared a number of cultural traits along with their linguistic similarities. The Algonquian tribal languages differed from one another and may not have been mutually intelligible. Unfortunately, many of the original American Indian languages are extinct. Linguists think the closest extant (or living) Algonquian language to that of the Powhatan language is Delaware, a language spoken by the Lenni Lenape Nation. Language revival is of great interest to those tribes who have lost their indigenous languages. Tribes in the western part of the state, such as the ancestors of the Monacan tribe, were not part of the Powhatan political organization and probably did not speak an Algonquian language.

John Smith's famous 1612 map of Virginia (see pages 22-23) shows the locations of many Indian villages. Smith indicates the Nansemond Tribe's four principle villages — Nand-sa-mund, Mat-ta-nock, Teracosick and Man-tough-que-men-o — were located on both sides of the Nansemond River, south of the James River, near present-day Chuckatuck. The Nansemonds also used the resources of the Great Dismal Swamp as well as the riverine resources of the Suffolk area. Most of the members of the present-day Nansemond tribe still reside in the same general area that was once home to their ancestors.

Some Nansemonds claim descent from the 1638 marriage of John Bass and Kesiah Elizabeth Tucker, the daughter of a Nansemond leader, who converted to Christianity. Chief Perry indicates, "Anyone seeking membership in the tribe today must submit supporting genealogical evidence which clearly shows 'family ties' to the established tribal lineages. The Nansemonds rely on three main records; a book written by Albert Bell entitled *The Bass Family of the South*, a bible, and a sermon book that the tribe has in its possession. People seeking membership in the Virginia tribes must search out their own genealogies. I suggest they start with court records of family members."

While searching for his own roots, Chief Emer-

Most of the members of the present-day Nansemond Tribe still reside in the same general area that was once home to their ancestors.

TRIBAL GENEALOGY

Smith, John. GENERAL HISTOIRE OF VIRGINIA (London 1624), Manuscripts and Rare Books Dept., Swem Library, College of William and Mary.

We're Still Here

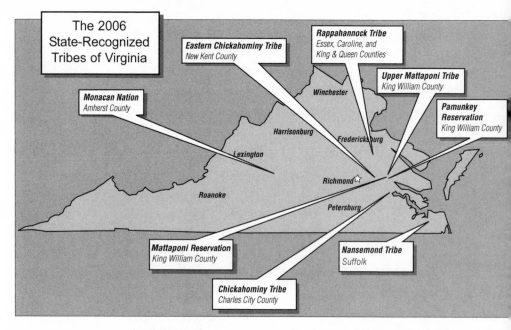

The 2006 State-Recognized Tribes of Virginia

Eastern Chickahominy Tribe
New Kent County

Rappahannock Tribe
Essex, Caroline, and
King & Queen Counties

Upper Mattaponi Tribe
King William County

Monacan Nation
Amherst County

Pamunkey
Reservation
King William County

Winchester

Harrisonburg

Fredericksburg

Lexington

Richmond

Roanoke

Petersburg

Mattaponi Reservation
King William County

Nansemond Tribe
Suffolk

Chickahominy Tribe
Charles City County

itus Perry became an authority on Nansemond history and compiled a list of important dates and significant events for a 1988 tribal homecoming. Registers from the Indiana Methodist Church, along with the fieldnotes and observations made by anthropologists who visited the descendants of the Powhatan tribes during the early 1900s, were also gathered by him and used for the state-recognition application. As an indication of his stature in the Virginia Indian community, Chief Emeritus Perry is often consulted on matters of Powhatan history.

Historical knowledge can be a sacred commodity among Native Americans. Dr. Linwood Custalow, physician and a member of the Mattaponi Tribe in Virginia, knows that sacred or privileged knowledge is not for general consumption. Dr. Custalow is one of the founding members of the Association of American Indian Physicians and a man who is educated in the traditional American Indian sense. He has the responsibility of keeping and passing on the Mattaponi tribal history to other members of the tribe. "Before the Europeans arrived on our lands, the Powhatan tribes had priests whose responsibility it was to remember and pass on historical and religious knowledge to the succeeding generations of priests. Powhatan society was hierarchical and the priests had a great deal of power. In contemporary American society we think that everyone should have access to all information. This notion was not held by our ancestors. Only select individuals had the right to know ritual and sacred knowledge. Such individuals were carefully chosen and trained. This was a serious responsibility," says Dr. Custalow.

In the 1750s the Mattaponi Tribe was converted to Christianity by a Baptist preacher named Bradby. This conversion forced the Mattaponi to do away with their traditional culture, clothing and language, but resulted in the survival of the people. Dr. Custalow believes a similar pattern occurred all over Virginia; native people who did not give up their traditional culture could be forced from their homes. "As the traditional priesthood was destroyed, the priests began to hand over their oral traditions and history to the political heads of the tribes — the tribal commanders. The customary way of passing on the tribe's oral history broke down. Tribal commanders or the chiefs now had the responsibility of maintaining both political leadership and tribal history. This was a change to our traditional cultural practices and ways of keeping our history," says Dr. Custalow.

The reservation tribes, the Mattaponi and Pamunkey, were more successful in holding on to tribal stories and ritual knowledge because they were able to maintain their political structures. Tribes who lost their land holdings had difficulty keeping traditions alive. Over time, with the decline of the traditional priesthood, tribal history was concentrated in the hands of fewer and fewer individuals. During the pre-Contact Period there were many priests, but after the eighteenth century

In the 1750s the Mattaponi Tribe was converted to Christianity.

RELIGIOUS CONVERSION

Tribes who lost their land holdings had difficulty keeping traditions alive.

the priests were gone and only a handful of political leaders were able to keep their tribal histories alive.

"We've held on to our Mattaponi Reservation," adds Dr. Custalow with a sense of both pride and responsibility as the keeper of tribal history. "However, what we have is just the central part of the village site. We used to hunt and farm in the area, and our sacred places are all around us. Our people are still here, and we would like an accurate account of our history to be known."

Agreeing with Chief Emeritus Perry's view that the history written in textbooks is "slanted," Dr. Custalow believes much of what is written in standard textbooks about Virginia Indians is inaccurate or at best misinterpreted. For years historians have relied on the writings of English settlers such as John Smith and William Strachey, and the late 16th-century watercolors and drawings of John White to reconstruct the landscape, environment and native lifeways of Virginia. Chief Emeritus Perry and Dr. Custalow believe the English sources do not provide a complete picture of the Powhatan tribes at the time of colonization. They maintain that the teaching of American history, which typically begins with European settlers occupying the "vacant lands" of North America, has done much damage to the general understanding of the diversity of American Indian cultures. School curricula should stress that North America was home to millions of American Indians in 1492. "I would like the term 'First Americans' to be used for our people," says Dr. Custalow. "Indian is not a correct name for us. It was used because Columbus thought his ships had brought him close to India. Many of our people do not like the term 'Native American' because anyone born in this country is a native-born American. I think calling us 'First Americans' would be more accurate."

North America was home to millions of American Indians in 1492.

There are also differing opinions regarding the peopling of North and South America. The migration of the First Americans from Asia to North America is said to have taken place during the last ice age, approximately 20,000 years ago. Some members of the American Indian and scholarly communities are now questioning the time frame and method of arrival of this migration. Some archaeologists think an earlier date is more likely for the arrival of the ancestors of today's American Indian people. In addition to the theory that during the last ice age people migrated across the exposed Bering Straits land bridge, some scholars are considering the possibility that some groups came to North America in boats. The questions surrounding the peopling of the "New World" may not be answered any time soon. It is likely that much of the evidence for solving this question lies in archaeological sites currently buried under the waters of the Bering Sea and along the coastline of the continents. Also, the oral histories of some tribes reference the creation of their ancestors on this continent. Therefore, some tribes completely reject the story of an ice-age migration to explain their presence in North America.

Few people understand the amount of diversity that existed in American Indian culture prior to 1492. Until recently, American Indians have been presented in books, literature and film as representing a single group of people, with very little emphasis placed on the distinguishing characteristics of their respective tribes. Since images from the Plains Indians are the dominant stereotype used for all other Indian groups, most people think of Indians as living in tepees and riding horses. This, of course, is not true. Tepees or skin-covered conical-shaped lodges were typically constructed by non-sedentary groups. Tepees were easy to put up and take down, and as such were the ideal home for Plains Indians who followed the buffalo herds on horseback and moved

HOUSING & TRANSPORTATION

their villages frequently. Virginia Indians lived in houses called *yehakins*, which were made of dried grass mats sewn together over bent tree saplings. Yehakins suited the more sedentary lifestyle of Indians who lived in villages close to their agricultural fields.

As with housing, the relationship between horses and American Indians has been misunderstood. The horse once lived in North America, but became extinct thousands of years ago. There is no evidence that ancient North Americans domesticated the horse, but they may have used it as a food source. The horse was reintroduced to North America in the 16th century when Spanish settlers brought them to Mexico and New Mexico. Like American Indians elsewhere on the continent, the Indians of Virginia did not have access to horses until they managed to obtain them years after the Europeans arrived in North America. Canoes hollowed out from logs were the preferred means of transportation for Indians in the Tidewater region and along the east coast. The extensive forests in the Eastern Woodlands provided the raw materials for canoes, which were

As documented in this Theodore DeBry engraving, canoes hollowed out from logs were the preferred means of transportation for Indians in the Tidewater region and along the East Coast.

made by setting fires to hollow out the centers of the logs. The fires were watched carefully to avoid burning a hole in the bottom of the canoe, and the cooled ash was scooped out using shells. The extensive waterway systems were easily navigated by dug-out canoes; they were used for more than transportation. The First Americans used the canoes for fishing and gathering edible plants that grew along the shore.

Many Virginia Indians hope the omnipresent presentation of American Indians in books and popular culture is changing. Today, American Indians are taking an active role in the retelling of their own histories. They are challenging some of the "official versions" of American history, such as the depiction of European colonizers as successful invaders as a result of their superior culture and technology. To some extent, the English survived the early years in Virginia because of the food and assistance that native peoples provided to them.

Chief Emeritus Perry recounts the details of an interaction between the Nansemond and John Smith. When John Smith and his men approached the Nansemond villages in August of 1608, there were nearly 1,000 acres under cultivation and a great amount of stored corn on Dumpling Island. This visit resulted in the commencement of hostilities between the English and the Nansemond people with Smith's men gaining the upper hand in the altercation. The incident ended after the English destroyed several Nansemond canoes and demanded the chief's weapons (bows and arrows), a chain of pearls and a payment of 400 bushels of corn. John Smith and his men indicated they would destroy the village, remaining canoes, and crops, and burn the Nansemonds' houses if the tribe refused to comply with their demands. The natives agreed to Smith's demands and watched as the English took most of the Nansemond corn back to the Jamestown settlement. The English returned to the Nansemond territory the following month to collect the remaining corn.

Relations between the Nansemond and the English continued to deteriorate when the English attempted to barter with the Nansemonds for control of Dumpling Island. The Jamestown settlers, in an effort to expand their settlement, sought fertile land and a secure site on which to establish a plantation. The settlers thought the Nansemond-controlled Dumpling Island would be an ideal location for their plantation. In a second violent action against the Nansemond, Captain Percy and Captain Martin directed English settlers to seize Dumpling Island. The English destroyed the temples and burial sites of the Nansemond leaders, referred to as "Kings" by the British. All houses and religious sites were ransacked for any valuables such as pearls and copper ornaments kept with the bodies of the leaders. Chief Emeritus Perry maintains the English continued to harass the Nansemonds throughout most of the 17th century, especially after the Nansemonds participated in the two uprisings against the settlers in 1622 and 1644. As early as 1664, land was surveyed by the colonial government and set aside for the Nansemonds.

"The tribe managed to hold on to some of their lands until 1792. The petition filed to sell the remaining land holdings of the Nansemond was probably illegal and by law should never have taken place. But that's another sad story, and I'm not sure that people are ready to hear about that part of our Virginia history," he says.

As an indication that views of history are beginning to change, Chief Emeritus Perry recalls, "In 1988, at the Nansemond Homecoming, a replica of the ship, Godspeed, sailed to Dumpling Island from the Jamestown Settlement in Williamsburg. On board were some of the museum's interpreters in 17th-century

DUMPLING ISLAND

Indian uprisings occurred in 1622 and 1644.

dress. They presented our chief with four bushels of corn. It was the symbolic repayment of the 400 bushels of corn which John Smith and his men demanded from our ancestors in 1608. It was a long time in coming."

Chapter 3

A Family Secret

Bernard Beverly spent part of his childhood in a log cabin in Amherst County, Virginia. There was no electricity, no indoor plumbing, and very little heat in the winter. Some mornings they woke up to find the water in the wash basin frozen.

Hard as it was to grow up poor, things became worse for the Beverly family and all other Indians when the Virginia General Assembly passed the Racial Integrity Act in 1924. Spearheaded by John Powell and Earnest Sevier Cox, founders of the Anglo-Saxon Clubs of America, and Walter Ashby Plecker, the first Registrar of Vital Statistics, this act made it impossible for anyone to be listed as "Indian" on any official record. Anyone who could not prove himself "white" was classified as "colored" on birth records, marriage licenses, and death certificates. Ironically, this was the same year American Indians were given American citizenship.

Many who lived around Bear Mountain, as Bernard's family did, used a local midwife partially because she would record "Indian" on birth certificates since the hospitals would not. But where the government had control, such as deciding which schools children would attend, the law was enforced.

Although he couldn't do anything about the Indians who lived on the reservations, Plecker set out to

> The Virginia General Assembly passed the Racial Integrity Act in 1924.

> That same year, American Indians were granted United States citizenship.

RACIAL INTEGRITY

prove that most people who claimed to be Indian were not. He compiled "hit lists" of names of families that had a history of being Indian and sent these out to hospitals and schools; they were not to be admitted to white facilities. He even added notes to the back of birth records that listed the child as Indian saying that Indian was not correct and the child should be regarded as "colored."

To escape these policies, many families left Virginia and settled in the surrounding states. The Beverlys moved to West Virginia. Their father also changed their name to Belvin, and as far as everyone was concerned the new family from Virginia was white.

Things were not always easy in West Virginia either. Bernard remembers, "My brother, Harry, and I were always getting into fights. We were much darker than most of the other kids, so some of the boys called us the N-word. We wondered why we didn't look like all the other kids. In addition to being dark, Harry had features associated with Indians you see out West. He insisted he was a Cherokee Indian, but I wasn't sure. I remember one day when mother was putting metholaid on my cuts after a fight, I came right out and asked her. I said, 'Mom, are we Indians?' she looked up at me and said, 'Yes, but it's not something we're proud of.'"

And it wasn't something they talked about with their younger sister, Mary, either. The youngest of the 13 children, her skin was so light that the white children in school did not question her heritage; they accepted her as one of them. No one in her family told her any different.

Looking back, Mary remembered asking her mother why Harry was so dark. She said, "Mother answered that she stayed out in the sun too much when she was carrying him, and that he was marked." Mary wasn't sure she understood that answer, but the question seemed to irritate her mother so she never brought the subject up again. As she said, "My parents never wanted to talk about anything, except the Bible."

As a result Mary grew up in the white man's world, thinking she was white. It was not until both parents were dead that she remembered hearing whispers that her mother was an Indian, and that they might be associated with the Cherokee people. She was 40 years old before she learned the truth of her heritage from an aunt in Maryland. Mary said, "She told me my mother and father were Monacan Indians, and that there was a tribe in Virginia, and a book about them called *Indian Island* which included a lot of information about Monacan families and ancestry. When I learned this, I was thrilled. It was like learning I had a complete new family."

The Racial Integrity Law was finally repealed in 1968.

Plecker remained in office until 1946. After he retired, the state began to end its harassment of Indians. But it was not until 1968 that the Racial Integrity Law was repealed. It was struck down as unconstitutional by the U.S. Supreme Court in the case Loving v. Loving.

After that, for a fee, Indians could receive a copy of their birth certificate listing their race as Indian, with the "Plecker note" removed from the back.

Even today the harm that Plecker did to Virginia's Indians is still felt as one person after another recalls that they did not know that they were of Indian heritage until their father or mother was on their deathbed. In some families it was a secret they were afraid to reveal.

Of course not all Indians left Virginia; some stayed and tried to fight the injustices. Others simply melted into the background and waited for things to change.

Plecker's policies have been called "eugenic homicide." He wrote many letters to officials trying to

PLECKER'S POLICIES

convince them that there were no true Indians in Virginia. In a letter written in April of 1943 to John Collier, Commissioner of Indian Affairs in Washington, D.C., Plecker said, "Send a representative to Virginia to examine the mass of original information and pedigree charts accumulated, showing the racial origin of the mixed breeds trying to pass as Indian."

As Bernard says, "I know other races, especially blacks, have had a hard time. But fortunately nobody ever tried to deny them their heritage. Nobody ever tried to deny they existed."

Eventually Mary and her brothers and sisters reconnected with their Monacan relatives. When they visited the church on Bear Mountain where many of the Monacan Tribe worshiped, Bernard said he was home. "I walked into that church and looked into their eyes, and knew they were family."

Bernard now lives in Texas and uses the name Beverly once again. Since they started learning about their Monacan heritage, they have become active in Monacan tribal activities. At a recent homecoming in West Virginia, Bernard was elected chief of the West Virginia branch of the Monacan Tribe.

Mary was asked by the Chief of the Monacan Nation, Kenneth Branham, to represent the tribe on the Virginia Council on Indians. She was appointed to the Council by Governor George Allen in 1995, and reappointed for a second term in 1998 by

Chief Kenneth Branham of the Monacan Indian Nation at the Monacan Homecoming.

HERITAGE

Governor Jim Gilmore. In 1997 Mary and other Monacan Indians approached the Council and said they felt it was not fair for Indians to have to pay to have their birth records corrected when it was the state, through Plecker, that made them incorrect in the first place. In a large family like Mary's, the fee became a burden.

To remedy this situation, Delegate Harvey Morgan sponsored HB2889 which allows the records for any Indian born in Virginia to be changed free of charge. When the bill was passed, Governor Allen wrote to Mary stating, *"This bill enables any American Indian born in Virginia, whose certified birth record contains an incorrect racial designation and was filed before July 1, 1960, to receive a copy of a corrected copy at no cost. A 1924 Racial Integrity Law resulted in inaccurate birth records that listed many American Indians as colored or white. Although this law was struck down, thousands of Virginia Indians are left with inaccurate birth records. This law gives proper recognition to Virginia's American Indians and corrects a long-standing wrongful practice."*

During Mary's second term on the Council on Indians she served as secretary. After her term on the Council expired she continued to work for her tribe as well as all Virginia Indians in various roles.

After her unfortunate death in April, 2003, Monacan Chief Branham said, "Without Mary we sometimes feel a little lost. She kept us informed on what was going on in Richmond, as well as what was happening in Washington with federal recognition. She worked tirelessly for us all, and made the three hour drive from Richmond to Amherst to attend our tribal council meetings every month. I would say she was probably in the top layer of leadership in the Monacan Nation. If she had lived here in the area, I'm sure the people would have elected her to be on our tribal council."

Anyone who knew Mary admired her devotion to

the indigenous people of Virginia including Senator George Allen who wrote the following to Mary's husband Al Wade after her death, "We all will greatly miss

Mary's wise and dignified counsel. She has always been a valued advisor to me since the days when I was Governor. One of the best decisions I ever made was appointing her to the Virginia Council on Indians.

Due to her thoughtful initiatives, Virginia Indians are treated with the respect and dignity that had been denied them for many generations."

Susan Allen, Governor Allen, and Mary Wadein 2000.

In 2005 in celebration of Women's History Month, the Virginia Foundation for Women honored eight women for their accomplishments and important contributions. Mary was chosen for her achievements as a civic activist. In honoring Mary they pointed out her accomplishments on the Virginia Council on Indians, her work as the founding president of the Virginia Indian Tribal Alliance for Life, and her participation in the Virginia Cultural Network, which was planning the 2007 commemoration of the settlement of Jamestown. It was also noted that she was instrumental in getting Senator George Allen and Representative James P. Moran to introduce legislation to extend federal recognition to six Indian tribes in Virginia, and that she worked tirelessly as the liaison between the tribes and as a lobbyist for the passage of the legislation which is still pending.

Today those who are interested in finding out if they have ties to the Monacan Indians can visit the museum in Amherst County where they have collected records and books to help people with their genealogical research.

GOVERNOR ALLEN

courtesy office of Senator George Allen

Chapter 4

Native Organizations

"The Commonwealth of Virginia has done well to create the Virginia Council on Indians (VCI) and make us a state agency," declares Gene Adkins, Assistant Chief of the Eastern Chickahominy Tribe, and their representative to the 2000 Virginia Council on Indians. The VCI was established in 1983 as an outgrowth of the state recognition process. Initially, six tribes were granted formal recognition in the Commonwealth, adding two more by 1990. Waiting for recognition by the state certainly took a long time — in fact the time frame must be measured in centuries. Even though Assistant Chief Adkins believes that Virginia Indians have "historically been treated badly" by non-Indians, he is quick to add

Members of the Virginia Council on Indians meeting at the capitol in 2004.

The Virginia Council on Indians was establishedin 1983.

"dwelling on the past doesn't help us to solve our problems in the present. The Council exists now to enable us to do things for tribes, and this is a great thing."

The Council reports directly to the Secretary of Health and Human Resources. Each of the Council's 13 members is appointed to three-year terms by the governor. There are representatives from each of the state recognized tribes, two Indian at-large seats, one citizen at-large member, and one member from the House of Delegates and the Virginia Senate. All members work as volunteers.

Karenne Wood of the Monacan Indian Nation is the 2005 chair of the VCI. She says, "The Virginia Council on Indians speaks in support of the 4,000 members of the indigenous Virginia tribes, the tribal chiefs, and also on behalf of the more than 16,000 American Indians who currently reside in Virginia. We feel that the VCI has become a progressive, proactive organization during the years since its formation, and we see its role as continuing to advise the governor's office and state legislature about issues of concern to Indian people, as well as taking a strong stand that Indian people are entirely capable of telling our own stories and articulating our own histories as the experts on our communities. Our histories are proud ones, and we are continuing to contribute to the growth and progress of the Commonwealth and to this nation, as we have since its beginning almost 40 years ago."

But Virginia Indians are still facing problems. When asked to state what he thinks their main problem is today, Gene's response is clear. "It's the lack of federal recognition for Virginia Indians."

After serving on the Council on Indians, Gene served as the president of VITAL, Virginia Indian Tribal Alliance for Life. The late Mary Wade was the first president of VITAL and along with Chiefs of the state recognized tribes and other Indian leaders, like Gene, organized the group in May, 2001 as a non-profit organization for political purposes. The group has been asking the United States Congress to grant Historic Federal Recognition to six of the eight state-recognized Indian tribes in Virginia. The General Assembly of the Commonwealth passed a resolution in 1999 which requested the U.S. Congressional Delegation of Virginia to take the necessary action to help Virginia Indians get the recognition they deserve.

On May 7, 2003 Representative James P. Moran introduced H.R. 1938 The Thomasina E. Jordan Indian Tribes of Virginia Federal Recognition Act to extend federal recognition to the Chickahominy Indian Tribe, the Chickahominy Indian Tribe — Eastern Division, The Upper Mattaponi Tribe, The Rappahannock Tribe, Inc., the Monacan Indian Nation and the Nansemond Indian Tribe. A Senate bill sponsored by Senator George Allen, R – Va. was also introduced that year.

The bills were not passed during the 108th Congress, so Senator George Allen, R-VA. introduced Senate bill 480, also known as the Thomasina E. Jordan Indian Tribes of Virginia Federal Recognition Act on March 1, 2005. A companion bill for the U. S. House of Representatives, sponsored by Representatives Jim Moran, D-VA., and Jo Ann Davis, R. Va. is also planned to be introduced.

Reginald W. Tupponce, Jr. a member of the Upper Mattaponi Tribe and current president of VITAL says, "The fact that the bill was introduced so early in the legislative year is a good sign. We are pretty optimistic that the bills will be passed soon." He adds, "It doesn't matter whether the glass is half full or half empty, I'm going to fill it up anyway. You have to believe. A lot of this is Faith. Faith kept us going all these years, and we have to believe that Congress and the whole country will finally do the right thing."

In Virginia, November is recognized as American Indian Month.

FEDERAL RECOGNITION

The tribes are pursuing federal recognition to qualify for educational scholarships, reclaim ancestral remains, qualify for low-interest business loans and have access to health benefits which are currently only available to federally recognized tribes. Those legislators who have opposed the bill often argued that it would allow the tribes to operate casinos in the state. Tribal leaders have never expressed interest in operating casinos, and the bill includes a provision that prohibits the tribes from utilizing the Federal Indian Gaming Act.

Members of VITAL have been going to Washington, D.C. on a regular basis to speak with congressional aides and members to discuss the bill. As Tupponce says, "As legislators and aides leave Washington, we have to go and tell our story all over again. VITAL's goals are to educate not just Congress, but people in the communities. It is a grass roots organization, and we have been holding many events, pow wows and festivals to inform people of our goals and aims, and to raise money to continue our educational efforts."

However, taking a public stand on political issues isn't always easy for Indian people. As Assistant Chief Adkins says, "Being an Indian person is not easy. We have been held back, and in the past people looked down on us. I was a shy person who kept my own identity to myself. But being a member of the Council on Indians changed me. I have learned not to be afraid to speak up, and how to do what is needed at the state capital. All the Council members have grown personally because we have been working on behalf of others in our community."

Another former VCI member, Arlene Giffel who represented the Upper Mattaponi Tribe, in 2000 echoed his sentiments. "Thomasina Jordan, our late Council Chairwoman was an excellent leader. Thomasina pushed me to do more on the Council and to get involved with the needs of the tribes. Since being on the Council I've learned more about my Indian heritage and I feel I've contributed to others. Serving Indian people in this way has enriched my life," says Arlene. She feels the VCI has accomplished a great deal since 1983. "The Council has worked for the designation of American Indian Month in the Commonwealth, which is celebrated each November, and the special acknowledgment of the Wednesday prior to Thanksgiving as American Indian Day. This corresponds to the day when the Pamunkey and Mattaponi Tribes pay their taxes to the governor in a public ceremony at the capital. The public recognition of American Indian Month and Day helps to raise the public's awareness of Indian people in our state."

While the VCI is the only state-sanctioned organization dealing with Indian issues, they are not the only Indian-run problem-solving organization in Virginia. The United Indians of Virginia, or UIV, is another similar organization. It was established to improve educational opportunities for the young people of the tribes, and to provide a forum for communications among the tribes. Current Chair, Jerry Fortune, a Rappahannock Indian, says that UIV is currently undergoing changes.

In 1983, state recognition was granted to 6 tribes including 2 reservation tribes.

REWRITING HISTORY

Virginia Council on Indians members (left to right): Troy Adkins, Mary Wade, Lonnie Custalow, Gene Adkins in 1999.

But he says, "Our mission is still the same. We just have to find a new location for our meetings and offices."

Marvin Bradby, chief of the Eastern Chickahominy Tribe, and former chair of UIV, thinks education is of paramount importance to the youth of today. "Whenever I have the opportunity to talk to young people, either at tribal functions, or on other occasions, I tell them 'Your mind is your most valuable possession-educate it — it holds your future.' My goal is to educate our youth to the end that we must be able to take part in our society. Education is the key to that goal. We can't turn back the clock and go back to live like our ancestors did, but we can take an equal part in today's society to benefit not only our people, but our whole community." To this end the United Indians of Virginia has established a scholarship fund for Virginia's Indian youth. Most Indian leaders agree with the sentiments expressed by Chief Bradby.

"I've long been a proponent of education and have always encouraged our young people to get as much education as possible," says Stephen R. Adkins, Chief of the Chickahominy Tribe. Leading by example, Chief Adkins graduated from junior college at 19, and went to work for E.I. Dupont in 1965. In 1971 he enrolled at the Virginia Commonwealth University and worked to complete a B.S. in Business Administration. Since then he has served on the Charles City County School Board.

Chief Adkins recalls, "I was on the school board and was looking at the criteria for a federal program called Title IV, also known as the Indian Education Act. One of the criterion was that a tribe be state or federally recognized. I found that our tribe was neither federally nor state recognized. That shouldn't have been a surprise to me, but it was. Then an Assistant Chief, Adkins took this message to the tribal council, and they agreed to spearheaded a drive for state recognition. Some older

The Governor's Conference on Indian Affairs is held each March.

members of the tribe weren't for it. My dad and his dad were brought up saying, 'Don't make too much noise or you'll lose what you have.' In other words, 'Be quiet, mind your business. Don't make waves.' I can understand that because in the past so much has been taken from them. Now here was this young radical named Steve Adkins saying, 'Let's go for it.' So to participate in educational programs, we went after state recognition."

After working hard to assemble the supporting documentary records to establish state recognition, the Chickahominy Tribe and five other Virginia tribes, including the two reservation tribes — the Mattaponi and Pamunkey, were granted state recognition on March 25, 1983. The Chickahominy Tribe now receives federal funds administered by the Charles City County School Board for an educational program at the Chickahominy Tribal Center. Children come on Saturdays to learn the history of their tribe, as well as traditional crafts and dances. There is an open house each year for members of the community and the school board to observe what is being accomplished in those classes.

Chief Adkins often gives talks to school groups in order to educate them about Virginia Indian history and culture. "A lot of the kids still think we are as the movies have shown us. They kind of romanticize us. I let them know we are real people competing in the market place along with everyone else. We have the same challenges in life that other people do; maybe more than some and less than some. We have an interest in our children getting a good education and a strong Christian ethic. I tell the students, we got a raw deal in the past, but no one in this audience has dealt me a raw deal. Some legislators still want to 'keep us in our place.' But I think most people would like to see us get a fair shake."

Chief Adkins adds, "I think the history taught in

AMERICAN INDIAN SOCIETY

schools is off base. To depict people who were defending their homes and families as savages is wrong, and that bothers me. We need to go back and put some energy into getting the history books straight. Now they are slanted in favor of the folks who wrote them, and they weren't Indians. I don't know what history would look like if an Indian had written it. Whoever has the pen in hand is bound to let some subjectivity creep into their work, but I would like to think I could be objective.

There are also several inter-tribal organizations whose function are primarily social, but also serve the Indian community in supportive ways which help to solve problems for Native Americans in the area. Mitchell Bush, founding member of one such group, the American Indian Society or AIS, feels the intertribal organization functions as a community for Indian people in northern Virginia, the District of Columbia and Maryland, most of whom live far from their original tribal lands. "Many Indian people have moved away from their reservations to find work in urban areas. In some ways AIS is like the tribe they have back home. AIS has a volunteer public advocate who gets involved in situations on behalf of Indians. We look after one another, especially if someone is in some kind of special need, financial or otherwise. When non-Indians need help they go to a government agency, but Indian people rely on one another. We have our own type of sharing. Indian people are raised to be generous with one another. If you look after those in need, when it is your turn and you need help of some kind it will come back to you."

In 2003 Debora "Littlewing" Moore, a member of the Pamunkey Indian Tribe in King William County, organized a group known as the Intertribal Women's Circle. The group continues to grow and now members come from several other states as well as Virginia. Moore emphasizes that this is a non-political group, and was

Debora "Littlewing" Moore as ladies lead dancer at a VITAL pow wow.

formed to get Indian women together to share knowledge and native traditions, as well as to share concerns about educating others about their history and culture.

Moore says, "The need for tribal women to come together is essential to the survival of not only our artistic traditions, family stories and fellowship, but the survival of the tradition of having our women commune together. The young and old alike are taught to respect each other and self. Through fellowship and learning we keep a large part of our heritage alive with the hopes of continuance for many generations to come."

Members and leaders of these various groups have traveled to meetings in Washington and to tribes in other states to try to understand the different problems which Indian people face. Some feel that Indians in Virginia are in a relatively good position compared with those problems faced by other tribes around the United States.

"Putting problems into perspective is a good thing, but it doesn't mean we won't keep working to improve things." says Gene Adkins, "We're still here and we're not going away! We still have a long way to go, and I hope the Virginia Indians who follow us will be driven to continue working to improve things."

Chapter 5

Living In Two Worlds

Today, there are some Indians who feel they live in two worlds. During the week they dress in business attire and are undistinguishable from other businessmen and women. But other days they are involved in working for and with their individual tribes. Many weekends they don buckskin regalia and attend pow wows, tribal homecomings, or heritage festivals. They balance between the Indian world and the outside world.

Juanita Smith and Reeva Tilley are two such women. They come from different tribes, and were brought up in different ways. Yet each is deeply involved in her own tribe's affairs, as well as groups that represent many Virginia Indians.

Juanita (or Nita), whose Indian name is "She Who Hugs," was not brought up in the Indian world. Her grandmother, who was a Nansemond, did not want to be Indian. As Nita says, "In the twenties and thirties it was not popular to be Indian in Virginia. But I really don't know if that was the only reason she denied our Indian heritage. She never talked

Nita "She Who Hugs" Smith, Nansemond Tribe.

about it. Even so, mother knew she was Indian, but she didn't know what kind. It wasn't until 1990 or '91 that my cousin contacted me and told me that Oliver Perry had reorganized the Nansemond tribe and that I could join if I wanted to. That was how I learned I was a Nansemond."

Since many Nansemonds live in the Chesapeake area, that is where their tribal meetings are held. Nita and her husband, Pinky, who is an associate member of her tribe in addition to being an assistant chief of his own tribe, the Red Cedar Band of Southeastern Cherokee Council, Inc., attend all the meetings — even though it is a two-hour drive each way. She is also the Nansemond's representative to the Virginia Council on Indians, their alternate to the United Indians of Virginia, and on the speaker's bureau of UIV. The Smiths give ten to fifteen talks a year to school groups and others. Nita stated, "I learned about my tribe by reading books and some notes that Oliver Perry put together. I also talked to what elders I could. Before our former Chief Earl Bass died, he gave me a lot of information. I can remember him telling us that in the early days we were the granary. We fed the English. We stored our corn on Dumpling Island and traded it to the English, but eventually they just took it in raids on the island."

Nita is retired from the Commonwealth of Virginia Department of Corrections. Every weekend from February to November she and her husband attend pow wows in Virginia, Maryland, and North Carolina. "Sometimes we drive five hours to get to a pow wow, but it's worth it." She explains, "It rejuvenates me; it's just like going to church. It makes it possible for me to be able to handle the everyday world. To be able to dance and talk with my friends makes it possible for me to go back to work for another week."

Nita says that she would like to have grown up in

HERITAGE

LEARNING

the Indian world, but she finds that the things she is learning now are very rewarding. "Learning about Indians has made me see things in a different light than the way I was raised. I have learned to respect my elders and nature more. It's taught me a different way of life. Learning Indian ways has also helped me in my relationships at work. I've learned to be more tolerant of others."

There are four qualities that she says serve her well in both the Indian world and the everyday world: dependability, patience, love and generosity.

"I've also learned a lot from different tribes. All of the tribes will get around to the same point eventually, and that is that Indians have been persecuted in the past, and that really hasn't stopped. It's time the government realized that we are here, and we aren't going anywhere."

Not all of her five children have chosen to join the Nansemond Tribe, but her son, Keith, and daughter, Phyllis "Morning Sky" DeLong, have joined, and they are very active in Indian affairs. Phyllis has been honored by her tribe and others by being chosen to be the lead female dancer at pow wows.

Phyllis has two children, James Douglas "Strong Heart" and Rachel Nicole "Shining Star." She is teaching them the Indian way from little stories that teach about their heritage and basic customs. Some of the stories also teach them the way an Indian looks at creatures in nature, and the moon and sun.

Phyllis "Morning Sky" DeLong reads to her children, Rachel Nicole "Shining Star" and James Douglas "Strong Heart."

INDIAN SCHOOLS

As she says, "My son thanks the sunshine every day, and he thanks the nighttime. He was taught to thank the nighttime because it's a time for the earth and all creation to sleep to gain strength for the next day. As he gets older he'll learn more about the moon because it purifies some things. He'll learn about ceremonies to purify things." Phyllis continues, "I haven't actually learned everything myself. Every time I turn around there is something new to learn. In the beginning I was real naive about certain customs and ways. As soon as I can conceive it all, I can teach my children."

Both of her children were carried into pow wows before they were a year old. She says, "It's very important to me that the first circle they're brought into is the Nansemond pow wow. It shows how proud we are to be Nansemond, and it's a way to support the tribe by showing our tribal strength. They are Nansemond, too and they deserve to be there just as much as anyone."

Bill Tilley

Reeva "Rose Eagle" Tilley.

Reeva "Rose Eagle" Tilley, who is an Accounting Manager with the Department of Criminal Justice Services in Richmond, was raised surrounded by family and friends who were all Rappahannock Indians. Her grandmother was the teacher of the Rappahannock Indian School in Indian Neck in King and Queen County before it was closed.

Reeva's cousin, Faye Fortune, remembers going to that school. "Reeva's grandmother, Marion Rollins, taught us all in one room. She had grades one through five, and she divided us into sections. She had two or three desks in each corner. She knew all about our grandparents and great-grandparents, and how they lived years ago. At that time, most of them were farmers, and some raised pigs. She would tell us what they did. I went to that school until I was in fifth grade and then they sent us to Sharon Indian View School. When I was in the sixth grade, they closed all the Indian schools and I had to go to an all-white school."

Faye explained that life was a lot easier when they went to the Indian school. As she says, "We didn't really know about the outside world until we started going to the public schools. We lived here in the country and weren't in the public view. Where one of us went, we all went. When we had to go to Sharon Indian School it wasn't so bad, even though it was an hour's bus ride; it still was an Indian school. But at the white school the other children weren't allowed to play with us. The kids would

Faye Fortune and her son Jacob "Little Pony" Fortune-Deuber, Rappahannock Indians.

tell us, 'My mom and dad won't let me play with you.' Through the years some would be friends with us even though they knew their parents didn't want them to. When Central High School was integrated, they sent us there — that wasn't a piece of cake either. My school years weren't very good years."

By the time Reeva entered school, the Indian school was closed, and she attended the integrated public schools in Essex County. She says, "I never understood it then, but now I do. Our mother never allowed us to go home with other children from school unless they were family. And they were not allowed to come to our house either. She didn't want us socializing with people outside of the Indian community. I guess she didn't want us being hurt." She continues, "There were bad feelings towards us when we were in school. Our elementary time was horrible. We were harassed all the

INTEGRATION

time by both the black and the white students just because we were different. Today people are shocked when I tell them that, because they don't see a difference. But it was that way. We didn't dress differently, we didn't do anything differently, but they knew we were different — they knew we were Indian."

Reeva adds, "My sister, Charlene, and I were talking about how much we hated to go school because so many people picked on us. There were days when I didn't want to get up and go to school. I didn't do well in school because I hated it so. It was so difficult to be Indian, but we stood up for what we believed in. I believed in my heritage and that I should be proud of it. I never maliciously hurt anyone because of the color of their skin, and I did not appreciate them doing that to me."

Every time she thinks of school she thinks of what they went through every day of their lives. Reeva explains, "You know, the fights, the name calling. It was an atmosphere that made it so difficult when you should have been focusing on your academic studies. For example, I can remember when they started picking the princesses for Homecoming. By the time I got into 8th grade, they were picking a white princess and a black princess — so where did that leave me, the Indian? I had a lot of people saying, 'Reeva why don't you do this?'" She pauses, "Well they didn't call me Reeva in school, they called me Gail 'cause a lot of people didn't like the name Reeva. Gail was my middle name and it was easier to say. Anyway, I didn't try for the Homecoming princess because I couldn't be the Indian princess. So we never had an option — never."

Indian children may not face the same open harassment in schools today, but they are not taught much about Virginia Indians either. That is why many tribes, especially the Chickahominy and Rappahannock Tribes, have their own classes on weekends and after school.

Marie D. Fortune has been teaching Rappahannock Indian children at the Tribal Center for two years.
"We started with children ages two to ten-years-old so
they could learn the dances of their heritage. At first,
classes were just every Wednesday evening, but in the
summer we went to two days a week. They learn a few
Algonquian words, the history of our tribe, and crafts.
The craft lessons are all tied to a history lesson. For
example, in the old days the men caught fish with traps
that they wove, so after we talk about that the children
weave baskets with construction paper strips.

"I also teach them respect for their elders, and
that you have to work to get what you want. You have to
work together with your tribe.We also learn about the
other state tribes, and how to spell their names. Sometimes the young ones think the Rappahannocks are the
only Indians in the state."

Marie is raising three children herself, and she
says that it's confusing for them in public school. Some
of the other children tell them they are not Indians; that
there are no Indians. She says, "It's another world. My
middle son is real dark. He goes to school and there are
black children in school, and he comes home and says
'They're brown like me, how come they're not Indian?' I
tell him being an Indian is more than your skin color. It's
about your ancestors and what they fought for, and the
traditions that you've grown up with, like the special
songs and dances that have been passed down for generations. I hope that they will learn about the tribe, and
want to be involved in the tribe when they grow up. A lot
of times the outside world influences the young people,
and they go away. I would like all of the children to stay
and not be influenced by the outside world, because
without the children there's no future. That's what I'm
afraid of, we've had so many stay away and not come
back. Some have come back, but there are ones my age

MIS-EDUCATION

who have yet to come back. It may be because of money, or because they're not accepted as Indians. There are a lot of people who look down on Indians."

Reeva knows what Marie means. She says that all her life she has had to prove who she was. "You would never ask a black or a white person to prove who they are. But we have always had to prove that we were Indian and fight to be accepted. I was bitter then, but you know what? I think God had a plan for me, and has helped me through a lot of troubled times. Everything I went through in school, and my whole life, has just made me a stronger person. Now I know I'm a very capable person, and a professional. I'm going to use that strength to get what I want for myself and for the Indians of this state."

While she feels she didn't get the education she should have gotten because she hated school so much, at forty-three she began working towards her BA at Averett College. She has also just taken a course in lobbying to help in her position with the Virginia Council on Indians. She serves on the Rappahannock Tribal Council, is a Sergeant First Class in the Virginia Army National Guard, and was Chair of the Virginia Council on Indians.

When asked what she is teaching her daughter, Shannon "White Dove," she answered, "I teach her to be proud of who she is." Then she laughed and added, "I teach her that she's not to buy Indian jewelry or crafts from the white man. People who are not Indian should not be selling Indian crafts." But in a serious mood again she continued, "I teach her that anything is possible. If you want it bad enough, you can succeed. That's an important lesson for my daughter to learn, because even though my parents loved me, I don't feel that was instilled in me. I think they were just happy we graduated from high school."

Chapter 6

Caring For Those Who Have Gone Before

"The archaeological report on the Patawomeck Creek site raises some new questions about the route our ancestors took in settling this region," says Robert Green, Chief of the Patawomeck Band of Potomac Indians. "The latest excavation suggests that our ancestors may have traveled south along the Appalachian Mountains to the present-day Stafford County region. Also, some of the ceramics or pot shards found at the Patawomeck site are similar in design to ceramic pieces which have been excavated at village sites in upstate New York. Our ancestors' pottery is similar to some of the Iroquois pottery. We are wondering if our ancestors were related to those northern tribes or if they were trading partners of the Iroquois."

The descendants of the Patawomecks are considering seeking official state recognition from Virginia's General Assembly. In putting together their request for recognition, Chief Green and his band's tribal historian are compiling all relevant historical, genealogical, and archaeological information on the Potomac Indians. Since so much of traditional Virginia Indian culture has been lost during the past four centuries, Chief Green and other Native American leaders look to archaeology to fill in some of the missing pieces of the past. The indigenous peoples of the Americas maintained their

ANCESTORY

traditions through oral histories and storytelling. Prior to the arrival of the European settlers there were no written records created by American Indians north of Mexico; therefore, archaeology is an important tool in accurately recreating the past.

Beyond the search for information about the past, archaeology can help to evaluate the accuracy of the early writings of European settlers. The written records of John Smith and other settlers were concerned with military matters and the strength of the Powhatan chiefdom. The authors of these early documents were very interested in noting the locations of the Indian villages which they encountered or heard about from other tribes along the coastal areas. Archaeologists try to link the written information to the actual landscape and they have had some success in this regard. John Smith's map of Virginia (pages 22-23) seems to have been drawn with great care and accuracy, and archaeologists have made a careful study of this map and other 17th-century documents.

"What we do is to try to reconstruct the past by using a systematic approach in our archaeological excavations," says Martin Gallivan, Ph.D., archaeologist and assistant professor at the College of William & Mary. "When done correctly, archaeology can inform us about numerous aspects of Virginia Indian life in the pre-contact period. Since Virginia Indians did not leave us a written record, archaeology is an important way to reconstruct the past. In fact, where written records do exist, such as in those produced by the 17th-century settlers, archaeology can help us to determine their accuracy. If Smith writes about the Monacan Indians at a particular location and we uncover a site in that area, we as archaeologists look for other confirming information to determine as best we can the cultural affiliation of the site."

Many archaeologists feel that their work can have

a positive impact on contemporary Native American people. "Archaeology involves the recovery of artifacts from the past, not because of any intrinsic value of the objects but for the information which the site and the artifacts can provide for us," says Dr. Gallivan. Archaeologists are also interested in examining the ways in which the arrival of settlers to Virginia changed the lives of Indian people. "Before we can discuss culture change, we need to have a better idea of what village life was like when just the Indians were here. That's really my main interest."

Only a few of the English authors, such as William Strachey, George Percy, and Henry Spellman, described the settlement pattern of the villages, housing style, and subsistence practices of the Virginia Indians. A great deal of the information that many Native Americans and scholars would like to know about pre-contact Indian life is not addressed in early writings and thus archaeology is the only way to recover this information. Certain aspects of culture are harder to excavate. The early records mention very little about the belief system and religious practices of the native people of Virginia. It is worth noting that few direct quotes or statements made by Virginia Indians are recorded in these documents.

While the written records present the European view of Virginia's native people, archaeology can help us uncover the voice of the First Americans. Due to the humid climate of Virginia and its soil conditions, archaeological preservation favors artifacts and items such as hearths, post holes, storage pits, arrow points and ceramics. It is the goal of archaeologists to use artifacts to describe the native people's lifeways and technology. Often seeds of edible plants are preserved at archaeological sites. Seeds and other plant materials may be recovered through the process known as flotation, which involves "washing" or sifting dirt from an archaeological

ARTIFACTS

We're Still Here

Projectile points, some pre-historic and some from the historic period.

site in buckets of water. Flotation permits bits of plant material and bone to float to the surface of the bucket where it is scooped up and taken to a laboratory for identification and analysis.

Sometimes archaeological artifacts deemed to be particularly important may undergo restoration and conservation treatments to preserve them from loss. Recently, two dugout canoes were excavated in Virginia. Few canoes from the early 16th century have survived; therefore, these two canoes are very significant archaeological finds. Both of the canoes had survived in wet conditions, which helped to maintain their structural integrity, and they had to be dried very slowly. The canoes are being preserved by museum conservators who are working carefully to avoid damaging the wood during the restoration process. Interestingly, one of the canoes has been attributed to the Nansemond Tribe and is currently being cared for at the Isle of Wight Museum. The second canoe is on display at the Virginia Historical Society in Richmond, Virginia, in their exhibit "The

Few canoes from the early 16th century have survived.

Story of Virginia."

Reflecting on the importance of the canoe to the Nansemond Tribe, Chief Emeretus Oliver Perry remarks, "We look forward to the day when the Nansemond Tribe has a museum of our own where we can display the canoe and other objects from our culture. Knowing that our ancestors built this canoe centuries ago is a source of great pride among the tribe."

While some Virginia Indians view archaeology as a means of obtaining reliable information about the past, others see the methods of archaeology as intrusive and a violation of a people's sacred and human rights. There are members of the contemporary American Indian communities who view archaeology as a controversial subject. This is especially true when archaeologists uncover or disturb human remains. There is strong sentiment among the American Indian population as a whole against disturbing, removing, or examining human skeletal remains. In 1990 legislation was adopted by the United States Government to protect American Indian burial sites, funerary objects, sacred objects and objects of cultural patrimony. This legislation, the Native American Graves Protection and Repatriation Act, or NAGPRA, offers federally-recognized tribes a say in the disposition of human remains and other objects. It also gives federally-recognized tribes the opportunity to have certain objects and human remains repatriated (or returned) to the control of the tribes. It is then left to the members of those tribes to decide on matters of reburial of human remains or use of sacred objects.

Since NAGPRA is a federal law and Virginia's indigenous people do not currently have federal recognition, the state-recognized tribes of the Commonwealth fall outside the legal protection and repatriation rights of the law. Virginia Indians are aware that at least one of the nation's most prominent museums has human remains

> The Native American Graves Protection and Repatriation Act, or NAGPRA, offers federally- recognized tribes a say in the disposition of human remains and other objects.

that have been identified as those of Virginia Indians. Yet the legal transfer of these human remains for reburial in the Commonwealth is not required by law. Generally, institutions such as museums or universities are reluctant to deal with non-federally-recognized tribes. Under the federal law, the "cultural affiliation" of any human remains or artifacts should be established before a repatriation takes place. Museums and other institutions are hesitant to release human remains or sacred objects to any group claiming Indian descendant without federal recognition. Such complicated legal maneuvering offers little consolation to those Virginia Indians who feel passionately about reburying the remains of their ancestors while waiting for the lengthy process of federal recognition to be resolved.

There have, however, been several instances when Virginia Indians were able to rebury the bones of their ancestors. In 1993, Chief Emeritus Perry oversaw the reburial of eighteen remains from the Paspahegh Tribe that were disturbed by a housing construction crew. He says, "The Paspahegh village was part of Powhatan's chiefdom and was located four miles from the site of the original Jamestown Fort. Most people do not know that the settlers' own records indicate they destroyed the Indian village in 1610, killing many of the Indians including women and children. By using maps and colonial records, archaeologists concluded the human remains were culturally affiliated with the Paspahegh village, and they dated the remains to the 15th or 16th century. Members of the Virginia tribes helped to bless the new grave site with sage and sweet grass. We held a solemn and respectful reinterment ceremony."

In 1997, Chief Emeritus Perry was responsible for securing the remains of 64 Chesapeake Indians who lived and died long before the arrival of European settlers to North America. The remains were excavated by archaeologists over a period of several decades and had been held by the Virginia Department of Historic Resources. Chief Emeritus Perry arranged for the 64 individuals to be reburied in a reverent ceremony. The event took place at First Landing State Park in Virginia Beach, a setting close to the ancestral home of the Chesapeakes, and included the singing of traditional American Indian songs and a sacred pipe ceremony. "We have planted 19 dogwood trees and erected a cedar fence around the grave site. We plan to plant 700 periwinkle plants in a circle over the grave site since it is now a sacred site to our people," he says. The reburial of the Paspaheghs and the Chesapeakes were important events for contemporary Virginia Indians. These reburial ceremonies have served to strengthen the resolve of Virginia's Indian community with regard to this issue. The Monacan Tribe also held a reburial ceremony in 1998 on their ancestral land called Bear Mountain, in Amherst County.

As Virginia tribes look forward to federal recognition, they expect that the need to rebury more human remains will increase. Discussion has been ongoing between the tribes about the construction of a Memorial Park to support what they expect will be the return of more than 1,000 human remains currently housed in museum collections. The Memorial Park is not planned as a museum but rather a hallowed ground where the remains could be buried with dignity and honor, a nationally significant place.

Chapter 7

Werowocomoco:
The Past Comes to Light

"I'm really proud to be a part of this excavation and so are the other Board members," says Jeff Brown, Pamunkey Tribal Council Member and member of the Virginia Indian Advisory Board to the Werowocomoco archaeological project. Jeff along with representatives from the Mattaponi, Upper Mattaponi, Chickahominy, Nansemond, and Rappahannock Tribes are assisting archaeologists from the College of William & Mary and the Department of Historic Resources as they excavate the primary village of the Powhatan chiefdom located on the York River in Gloucester County, VA. The village named Werowocomoco was the seat of power for Wahunsensacah, widely known as Chief Powhatan, at the time of the arrival of the English in 1607. Wahunsensacah held the position of Mamana-towick, the Powhatan word for the most powerful civil leader of the chiefdom.

Jeff Brown (Pamunkey Tribe), and archaeologists Martin Gallivan and Dave Brown at Werowocomoco.

American Indian Resource Center, College of William & Mary

    Academic researchers and tribal members agree that the goals of the excavation are first to learn more about Powhatan society and second to learn more about the interaction between Natives and European settlers in the early years of the seventeenth century. The Werowocomoco excavation draws on archaeological evi-

65

We're Still Here

dence, primary source documents and contemporary Native commentary in order to address these research questions. Thus careful excavation of the site, detailed record keeping, precise cataloging of artifacts and interpretation of the data are essential components of this project.

The Virginia Indian Advisory Board meets regularly with the Werowocomoco Research Group team to discuss details of the project and to help establish policy and protocol for the excavation. Jeff notes, "This is the first time that tribal members have been directly involved in a archaeological project of this size and importance to our people here in Virginia."

A description of the Powhatan village of Werowocomoco is included in John Smith's *A True Relation* along with Smith's capture by Chief Powhatan's brother Opechancanogh. Smith's subsequent meeting with Chief Powhatan at Werowocomoco is part of this seventeenth century work. The village of Werowocomoco is the setting for the famous meeting between John Smith and Pocahontas. Interestingly, Smith does not mention his 'rescue' by the young Pocahontas until the publication of his book *The General History*. While there is great speculation by academics and others about the specifics of the Pocahontas/Smith story, many people remain interested in this aspect of Werowocomoco history.

The village of Werowocomoco was known to historians, anthropologists and native people through primary documents and oral tradition. Chief Powhatan removed himself from Werowocomoco to the village of Orapaks in 1609 to get away from the English settlers. Gradually this important place and its history receded from memory and mention in colonial records. In 1977 ceramic sherds and stone artifacts were collected from the surface of the site and the Virginia Department of Historic Resources registered the location as an official

The official archaeological site "44GL32" was recently identified as the historic Powhatan village of Werowocomoco.

Werowocomoco: The Past Comes to Light

archaeological site and gave it the number "44GL32". However, a comprehensive excavation of the site and its actual identification as the historic Powhatan village of Werowocomoco occurred only recently when the current landowners, Lynn and Bob Ripley, collected more artifacts from the site and agreed to host a major excavation in their backyard. Beginning in 2003 the College of William & Mary has held a four week field school on the property every summer. Undergraduate and graduate students from the Department of Anthropology have become part of the Ripley's extended family living on the property during the excavation. The Ripley's enthusiasm for the project and commitment to Native participation in the excavation has been a key factor in the success of the establishment of the Virginia Indian Advisory Board.

The collaboration between researchers and tribal members has grown to the point that in the summer of 2005 Jeff Brown joined the students for the entire field season by excavating, sharing his perspective on the project and adding freshly caught crabs to the students' dinner faire. During each of the summer excavations members of the tribes have been invited to the site to observe the progress of the excavation, the on-site processing of artifacts and to spend time with the students. Artifacts such as stone points, pieces of ceramics, beads and high status items such as copper are beginning to tell a story of trade between Natives and the English at Werowocomoco. As the excavation progresses, more definitive information will be available to the scholarly community, tribes and the general public.

Gloucester County classroom teachers have spent time at the site as well. Tribal leaders and archaeologists hope the teachers' on-site experience at Werowocomoco will enrich the teaching of Powhatan and early Virginia Colonial history to students locally and around the state.

Not only did the artifacts speak to Native occu-

These artifacts — ceramics, stone points and copper — are from the werowocomoco excavation.

Archaeologists are also interested in examining the ways in which the arrival of settlers to Virginia changed the lives of Indian people.

pation of the site during the early contact period, but examination of maps from the early seventeenth century, such as those drawn by Perdro Zuniga (1608), Robert Tindall (1608), and John Smith (1612) all place Werowocomoco on what is today the York River at Purton Bay. The evidence collected from the site combined with the primary documents from the Colonial era leave no doubt that the location of Werowocomoco is known with certainty.

The DHR and William & Mary Department of Anthropology partnership has received generous financial support from the Virginia Foundation for the Humanities and the National Endowment for the Humanities. Since the location of the village of Werowocomoco is private property access to the site is limited. However, the research team has created a website (powhatan.wm.edu) to aid in public outreach.

One aspect of this area's history now more clearly understood because of the excavation is that this village was inhabited for hundreds of years prior to the arrival of English settlers in coastal Virginia. The radiocarbon dating of charcoal samples from the site as well as the artifacts and features being uncovered in the excavation speak strongly to the presence of Native peoples long before European settlement. This aspect of the chronology or dating of the site appears to be of greatest interest to the contemporary Native community and confirms what many Powhatan tribal members always maintained. Powhatan history does not begin in 1607, but rather their ancestors inhabited the region for thousands of years before the arrival of the English. With the focus on the four hundredth anniversary of the founding of James Fort Powhatan tribal leaders are pleased to focus on aspects of their own history at Werowocomoco. "It's as if the site remained asleep...protected...until this current generation of Powhatan descendants were able to work with the archaeologists on this excavation." says Chief Anne Richardson of the Rappahannock Tribe. "This is not something that would have happened in years past. It is a blessing and a responsibility for our people to be part of the restoration of Powhatan history and culture at Werowocomoco."

Chapter 8

Pottery:
Our History in Clay

Firing pottery in an outdoor pit the way pre-historic Indians did is risky. As Pamunkey Indian Joyce "Pale Moon" Krigsvold says, "You've got to be careful when you fire outdoors. You can't fire in the winter because the temperature changes can cause a pot to break. Once I put the pots in the pit, I cover the fire with pine needles, green wood, or green leaves; anything that will cause smoke, because the clay changes color according to the amount of smoke. You never really know what color it's going to be. Sometimes it comes out real black, sometimes gray and black on one side, and sometimes you even get a brownish color. It's always a surprise."

Joyce and Mildred "Gentle Rain" Moore are carrying on the Pamunkey tradition of pottery making that began before the English settled Jamestown. But it may be coming to an end. In 1935 there were eighteen Indian men and women making pottery on the Pamunkey Reservation in King William County. By 1985 that number had dwindled to seven, and by 1998 there were only these two Indian potters left. There is some

Joyce "Pale Moon" Krigsvold, Pamunkey Tribe.

71

concern that this tradition that is so closely associated with Pamunkey Indian history may end with the current generation.

Mildred feels it is the only cultural tradition left among the Pamunkey people. She says, "Our language is already gone. Pottery is the only culture we have left."

Pottery, also referred to as ceramics, is important not only because of cultural traditions, but also because historians can often identify the time period, or area, the clay pieces came from. This can give them clues as to tribal movements and pre-contact, inter-tribal trade patterns. In addition it indicates trade patterns between the Indians and settlers.

The making of clay vessels is one of the elements that typifies the time period known to archaeologists as the Woodland Period (1200 B.C. – 1600 A.D.). Prior to this time, during the Archaic Period (8000 – 1200 B.C.), the bowls that they used were carved from

soapstone. If a site yields pottery, it probably dates to the Woodland Period or later.

The Pamunkey are particularly well-known for their pottery making because their work with the clay from the banks of the Pamunkey River has been continuous since pre-historic times. In their past, other Algonquian-speaking tribes, as well as the Iroquoian and Siouan Tribes located in Virginia, also used clay to make vessels for cooking and storage, as well as

The making of clay vessels is one of the elements that typifies the time period known to archaeologists as the Woodland Period.

CULTURAL TRADITION

Mildred "Gentle Rain" Moore, Pamunkey Tribe.

ceremonial objects.

Joyce learned to make pottery from her mother who is now deceased. She says, "The sad part is that the older ladies who know how to do the pottery are dying out, and no younger ones are learning."

These two Indian women not only fire their pottery using some of the same methods their ancestors did, but they also use clay from approximately the same location. Sadly it is getting harder and harder to find. Joyce says, "In the old days the women would show the men where to dig. It's kind of like gold. There are veins of clay in the riverbank. Now that all the older women are gone, we don't know where that best vein is. You can get clay, and the men still dig about twelve buckets of clay for us each time they dig, but it's a little sandier than it used to be. We've tried working with other clay, but we prefer our own. Ours is much better clay to work with. I'm not sure what makes it so much better than commercial clay. Maybe it's the elasticity, I don't know. Another thing is that our clay doesn't dry out as quickly as other clay."

Pinching together long ropes of clay to form vessels is the tradition known as the coil method of pottery-making.

Both women prepare the clay for pottery making as it has been done for hundreds of years. It is a skill that has been passed from generation to generation. First, they let the clay dry out and then break it into small pieces. The next step is to put it in water and soak it until it is the consistency of cream. Then it is strained to get all the rocks and debris out. Finally, it is poured over plaster bats to draw the water out of it until it is the consistency of dough. Then it can be kneaded and made into pots.

Mildred's mother did not work in clay, but her mother's sisters did. They worked in a building called the Pottery Workshop located behind the schoolhouse on the reservation. As a child Mildred remembers going to the workshop after school to watch her aunts work, and

Left: Historic pottery fragments (pieced back together) are filed at the Department of Historic Resources. Right: A vase by Mildred Moore in the Pottery School Tradition.

they showed her what to do with the clay.

During Mildred's childhood, in the 1940s, the Indian women were working in what is called the "Pottery School Tradition." This tradition began in 1932 when the state of Virginia initiated a plan to help the Pamunkey Indians develop their craft into a source of income. The State furnished the materials for a building to house the Pottery School and the Tribal Council furnished the labor to construct it. The state provided a teacher, William Ross, who happened to be non-Indian. He introduced changes that are still reflected in Pamunkey pottery. To increase the speed of manufacture, modern technology was introduced. Firing in a kiln and using glazes became part of the pottery-making process. The kiln provided a more uniform heat, and a method of cooling the pottery down slowly to reduce breakage. But the attractive shades of gray that occurred from the flames of the fire, the smoke, and the disintegrating wood were eliminated, and the pots that came out of the kiln were a uniform, brownish color. To make them more attractive, they began applying color to the bisque ware, and eventually began to cover the colors with a clear glaze that made the pots water repellent. Since painting pottery was not an historic tradition, the teacher taught them designs and pictographs taken from Southwestern Indian traditions. Today vessels are still decorated with two stories that are important to the Pamunkey people. One set of pictographs tells the story of Pocahontas and Capt. John Smith, and the other tells the story of the treaty that established the presentation of game in lieu of taxes to the governor of the colony. The Pamunkey still follow that tradition, although they now make their presentation to the governor of Virginia.

The second instructor, Frank Lutz, introduced the squeeze mold. The molds were made of clay or plaster of Paris from clay vessels or sculptures that were originally made by hand. By using molds the potters were able to reproduce several copies of the same vessel quickly. Some of the molds that were used have been passed down through the years and Mildred and Joyce occasionally use them today.

After the state stopped sending a teacher to the Pottery School, some of the potters went back to creating pottery using the traditional techniques.

Now, Joyce and Mildred make pottery in both the traditional and "Pottery School" styles. The vessels produced by traditional methods are called "blackware." These vessels are built by hand, usually using the coil method, and when dry to a leather-hard consistency are burnished with a stone or bone tool. Joyce still has the tool her mother used for burnishing. It was made from a deer's antler. After the vessel is burnished it is put in the kiln and fired slowly and at a low temperature to make it stronger and reduce the chance of breakage in the outdoor fire.

POTTERY CHANGES

We're Still Here

The clay used to make pottery during the Woodland Period was strengthened (or tempered) with crushed and burned shells, crushed steatite, river pebbles, or quartz sand. Archaeologists can analyze the type of tempering material to help them identify the area, or time period in which the pottery was made. Typically, cooking vessels had cone-shaped bottoms so that they could be set into the earthen hearth with the fire built around the sides or balanced on three stones over a fire. They were often decorated by a paddle wrapped with cord or cloth which was pressed into the damp clay. Since fabric from these prehistoric periods has not survived, the markings left by cloth paddles gives historians some idea about early textile making.

Around 1300 A.D. the Algonquian-speaking and Siouian-speaking Indians used similar methods to make and decorate their pots. However, the Iroquoian people made round-bottomed pots that curved in and then ended in a type of collar which was decorated with geometric designs, incisions, or cord-wrapped paddles.

When pre-historic pottery is found at an archaeological site in Virginia, it is usually turned over to the Department of Historic Resources in Richmond. That is where archaeologists catalogue and describe the artifacts. If the piece is going to go on exhibit, it goes into the lab for cleaning and repair.

Melba Myers, Conservator for the Department of Historic Resources, says, "In many of the pre-historic ceramics that we get, the physical material is usually in pretty good shape. All it needs is to be washed, but sometimes it is so soft and crumbly that even washing it with a toothbrush can damage it. If we receive several pieces of a vessel, we try to reconstruct it. We put them together and mend them. Sometimes we get pieces from a private collection. Some have been mended with glue that has turned brown, and we have to take that old glue off and redo the mend. We use special glue that will hold up under exhibition conditions, especially lights, but none of the repairs that we do are permanent. If better techniques or materials are discovered in a few years, we want to be able to reverse what we've done. That is why I document everything I do. I take pictures before and after I do anything, and write up what I've done including what kind of glue I used."

Some of the Indian pottery from the Department of Historic Resources is on display in the Virginia Historical Society's exhibit "The Story of Virginia."

Mildred sells both blackware and pieces in the Pottery School Tradition, in her little blue gift shop on the Pamunkey Indian Reservation.

The Pamunkey Museum on the reservation is one of the best places to learn about Indian pottery as they have a variety of vessels on display, as well as a video and exhibits which explain different types of temper, construction methods, and ways of decorating pieces.

Both styles of Joyce's pottery are available in the Pamunkey Museum, and some of her work, in the Pottery School Tradition, is also in Historic Jamestowne and Jamestown Settlement Gift Shops.

Other tribes such as the Mattaponi, Rappahannock, and Chickahominy have excellent potters who now display and sell their work at a variety of places. On the Mattaponi reservation some women have signs by their mailboxes indicating that they have pottery for sale in their homes, while other potters sell their work in booths at heritage fairs and pow wows. Pamunkey pottery is featured at the National Museum of the American Indian in Washington, D.C.

Chapter 9
Pow Wow: Gathering of the People

At the Mattaponi pow wow, Charlene Rollins, a Rappahannock Indian, and Wayne Adkins, a Chickahominy Indian, dance the Two Step. This is one of the few Indian dances where men and women dance together (1999).

"Before I enter the dance circle at a pow wow, I always pray ... giving thanks to the Creator for allowing us to gather, and in thanksgiving for His many blessings to our people." Troy Adkins of the Chickahominy Tribe finds participating in the pow wows of Virginia and neighboring states to be truly rewarding. Among Virginia Indians, Troy is a respected dancer, drummer and singer, and he enjoys celebrating his Chickahominy heritage and traditions at pow wows. However, according to Troy, what is most important about any pow wow is the gathering of Indian people, and the opportunity to see family and old friends and make new friends during the special time of celebration that is part of every pow wow.

The origin of pow wows is somewhat uncertain.

POW WOWS

79

We're Still Here

The word *pow wow* is most likely derived from the Algonquian word *pau wau* which referred to the gathering of medicine men for a curing ceremony. The modern pow wow is probably an outgrowth of the gatherings that were popular among Plains Indians tribes during the mid-to-late 19th century. Among the Plains tribes, men's warrior societies would enact dances to memorialize battles and feats of bravery. As the United States Government sought to assimilate Native Americans into the larger society, Indians were discouraged from holding pow wows and engaging in traditional dancing and drumming. In order to maintain their traditional dances and songs and avoid criticism from government officials, some tribes held pow wows that coincided with Fourth of July celebrations and other national holidays. This offered Native Americans a chance to dance in public without fear of receiving sanctions from the government.

During the late 19th and early 20th centuries, members of different tribes from around the country interacted with one another at government-sponsored boarding schools. While most Native Americans speak of boarding school in very negative ways due to the harsh treatment they received at these schools, there was a hidden benefit. The experience brought Indians from around the country in contact with one another. Many pow wow songs and dances were shared among the boarding-school students and taken back to their respective tribes upon returning home. These newly-learned songs and dances were incorporated into tribes' pow wow traditions. The post-World War II era saw a revival in American Indian pow wows as tribes held dances and celebrations for returning veteran tribal members.

Honoring veterans is still one of the central themes of every contemporary pow wow. American Indian veterans, especially those who have served in the

> Among the Plains tribes, men's warrior societies would re-enact dances to memorialize battles and feats of bravery.

> The post-World War II era saw a revival in American Indian pow wows as tribes held dances and celebrations for returning veteran tribal members.

American Indian veterans' color guard leads the Grand Entry at the inaugural Indian Pines pow wow.

military during times of war, often serve as members of the pow wow color guard. It is the duty of the color guard to bring the American flag, flags of other countries (particularly the Canadian flag), and any tribal flags into the dance circle for the pow wow's grand entry. The grand entry is a ceremonial parade during which the color guard, tribal chiefs, lead dancers, and all participants in regalia enter the dance circle. Once the flags are posted in a place of honor, the dancing gets underway.

Some tribes instituted an annual pow wow that functioned as a large family reunion or homecoming for the entire tribe. Originally, homecoming pow wows were for tribal members, and not public events. At least one tribe in Virginia used to hold pow wows exclusively for their own members. "Before the pow wows were public events, they were held at the private homes of tribal members. There was plenty of dancing, singing and cooking at these private pow wows where relatives got together. The Chickahominy tribe began holding a public, annual fall festival and pow wow in 1951," says Troy.

The Chickahominy Fall Festival Pow Wow is held during the last weekend in September. Troy has served as

GRAND ENTRY

We're Still Here

the coordinator of his tribe's pow wow committee and knows that organization and planning is key to holding a successful pow wow.

Edmund Adams, former Chief of the Upper Mattaponi Tribe, has seen pow wows in Virginia become more popular among the tribes and non-Indians in recent years. "There's a lot of hard work to be done in setting up and cleaning up after a pow wow. You have to have a lot of support from your tribal members. In many ways, hosting a pow wow can help pull a tribe together and make it a stronger group."

Earl Bass, the Assistant Chief of the Nansemond, has been a coordinator for his tribe's pow wow. "You have to begin planning a year in advance. The pow wow planning committee is very important to hosting a successful pow wow, but the most important people at the event are the participants. Every pow wow has a head male and female dancer and a Master of Ceremonies. The Master of Ceremonies has an educational function. It is the responsibility of the M.C. to announce each dance before the drumming and singing begins. This tells the dancers the type of song to expect and tells the audience what type of dance they will see. If an "intertribal"

Pow wow: Gathering of the People

dance is announced, members of any tribes present may enter the dance circle. If a men's traditional dance is announced, then only those men wearing men's traditional regalia may enter the dance circle. The same is true for other styles of dancing such as jingle dress dancers, ladies' traditional, ladies' fancy or shawl dancers and grass dancers. Sometimes special dances are announced to honor a tribal member either living or deceased. There is even a pow wow dance called the "two-step" which has its roots in square dancing. The two-step is just about the only dance where men and women dance together as partners. It is a special honor to be asked to be one of the lead dancers at a tribe's pow wow. The tribe makes a selection according to the personal qualities of an individual. While lead dancers have to know the different dances, they are also representing Indian people to the public and that is more important than anything else," explains Assistant Chief Bass.

Since the pow wows present a part of American Indian culture to the general public, the pow wow committee members approach planning the pow wow in a serious manner. Chief Edmund Adams feels that the location of his tribe's pow wow is very significant. "We hold our pow wow close to our old school and church grounds. Many of our tribal members have spe-

It is a special honor to be asked to be one of the head dancers at a tribe's pow wow.

There is even a pow wow dance called the "Two-Step" which has its roots in square dancing.

Preston Adkins, a Chickahominy Indian, often serves as Male Lead Dancer at pow wows. He is a traditional dancer.

cial memories associated with that piece of land. It's a time to have fun, but it's also very special for our tribe. It is really a time to show others who we are as Virginia Indian people."

There is also a spiritual side to the pow wow. Assistant Chief Bass says, "When you sit in a church you feel close to the Holy Spirit. When we dance at the pow wow we feel the Great Spirit is here. When you see hawks circling overhead while dancers are in the circle in their regalia, you know the Great Spirit is here."

Pow wow dancers refer to the special clothing that they wear for these events as regalia. An individual dancer may spend years making and assembling dance regalia, which includes everything from moccasins to a

REGALIA

As illustrated in this Theodore DeBry print of two Indian men, dancer's regalia may reflect an individual's lineage, tribal heritage or spiritual views.

headdress. A dancer's regalia may reflect an individual's lineage, tribal heritage or spiritual views; it's always individualistic. Regalia tends to reflect particular styles of dancing. Male dancers may wear feather bustles and dance in vigorous and athletic ways, while other men may prefer a more subdued style of dancing and wear regalia made of either cloth or buckskin. There are "grass dancers" who wear a distinctive regalia with colorful yarn to represent the tall grasses on the Northern Plains.

Like their male counterparts, women may wear either cloth or buckskin regalia. There are also women jingle dress dancers and fancy dancers. However, most women carry a shawl into the dance circle. It is not uncommon for a dancer to receive a gift of specific regalia items from family members or friends. These gifts are incorporated into dance regalia and have special value to the individual dancer.

Most importantly, many Native American children are brought into the dance circle when they are young and they are encouraged to participate in the pow wows as they grow up. This gives young people a sense of their ancestry. Jamie Ware-Jondreau, a Rappahannock Indian, was taught traditional American Indian dances by her parents. Jamie has brought her niece, Tashina, to pow wows for years and is continuing to pass on the traditions to her young daughter, Meno Kay. "This is how the children learn to be part of the community and to express their unique heritage," declares Jamie.

CHILDREN

Jacob "Little Pony" Fortune-Deuber dances at the 1999 Rappahannock Pow Wow.

"By incorporating the younger and older members of our community together, our children can begin to gain a sense of the long continuity of the American Indian community. Indian people are taught to think of future generations, and we do this by handing down our traditions to our children. We teach our children about the significance of the circle; our children learn to dance in a circle. We feel connected to the past and linked to our future as a people."

An important part of any pow wow is the drumming and singing. Virginia Indians are fortunate that a number of excellent Native American drum groups are active in the Commonwealth. Some, such as Lonnie Custalow's Mattaponi drum group, the former *Wahunsenacah*, have made recordings of their music. Lonnie has even composed original music for his drum. Lonnie's songs incorporate vocables, or sounds chanted in a rhythmic manner, along with words from native languages and English words. The songs are usually sung in a high pitch and a loud voice. Singing with a drum group is a physically demanding undertaking. The number of drummers and singers associated with a particular drum may vary, but as a general rule there are usually at least four members. Most drummers are also the singers and with rare exception, they are always male.

"The drum is viewed as 'female' by Native Americans and the drummers are male," says Bob Jondreau, Jamie Ware-Jondreau's husband and member of the Ojibwa Tribe of Michigan. Bob heads a drum group in Virginia known as Four Rivers. His drum group is composed of musicians who are members of tribes from other parts of the country. "Some of these young men live in Virginia because they are on active duty in the U.S. military and they are stationed here. Being part of a drum group helps them to maintain links with their American Indian cultural traditions and makes them feel like they

SINGING

are part of a family. Plus it's a way of sharing songs from one tribe to another. One drummer may be a member of the Lakota or Sioux Nation and he may know some different songs which he teaches to the rest of us."

Bob's drum members meet weekly to practice their songs. "It is a real commitment to be a member of an American Indian drum group. We sometimes have to travel around the state to perform at pow wows. You have to believe in what you are doing."

Bob feels that both Indian and non-Indian people are drawn to the sound of the drum because it represents the heartbeat of mother earth. "All people recognize that sound because it is the same sound you heard when you were growing in your mother's womb before you were born. The deep, rich sound of the American Indian drum is familiar to all people and it is comforting to listen to its beat."

No American Indian pow wow would be complete without fry bread and crafts. Visitors can get a taste of one of the more traditional American Indian foods —fry bread (see page 86 for recipe) at nearly every pow wow. American Indian artisans use the pow wows to showcase their jewelry, beadwork, and pottery skills. The pow wow is one of the best places in Virginia to shop for American Indian arts and crafts.

Mitchell Bush, an Onondaga tribal member from New York State, is a founding member of the American Indian Society (AIS). The American Indian Society holds an annual pow wow on their own property in Ruther Glen, Virginia. Mitchell emphasizes that non-Indians are always welcome at the state's pow wows; however, they should be aware of proper pow wow etiquette. "The Master of Ceremonies will announce the dances and indicate who is called to dance. Visitors should always respect the sacredness of the dance circle. It is inappropriate for non-Indians to enter the dance

DRUM GROUPS

Visitors can get a taste of one of the more traditional American Indian foods — fry bread, which is sold at nearly every pow wow.

We're Still Here

circle unless invited to do so by the Master of Ceremonies or another Native American dancer. If you are invited to join in a dance, you should enter the circle and walk or dance in a clockwise direction. Guests at any pow wow should always ask permission before taking any photographs of dancers in regalia or recording any singing or drumming. Most importantly, no one should ever touch the regalia of a dancer unless invited to do so. Pow wow regalia has personal meaning to the individual dancer and he or she may not want particular items of regalia to be handled. If you're not sure what to do, always ask," says Mitchell.

Being there is the best way to learn about the pow wow and America's first people. "It's about pride. The pow wow shows that we're still here!" says Assistant Chief Bass.

Chapter 10

Food Ways

Rebecca Costanzo

"I used to tell people that when I was growing up if you didn't kill it or grow it, you didn't eat it." Reeva Tilley, a Rappahannock Indian, continues, "People look at me now, and when I tell them that I've eaten rabbit, squirrel, and things like that they say, 'Gosh, I look at you in a different way now, Reeva.' When they see me dressed in pumps, the business suit — you know, the whole nine yards — they can't imagine that I ever lived that way."

The Rappahannock Indians used to live on the Rappahannock River, but over the years they were pushed back, and now live several miles from the river. But some, like Mark "Thunder Hawk" Fortune, Assis-

Delicious and bountiful basket of indigenous foods gathered at Jamestown Settlement's Powhatan Village.

HUNTING AND TRAPPING

tant Chief, still look to the river for food. He hunts snapping turtles as his ancestors did. "My dad passed these ways down to me, and his father taught him. I'm teaching my three boys, although they're still too young to get too close because the turtles are very dangerous if provoked. Some of the bigger ones are more than twelve inches across and very strong. It can take two or three people to get those big ones in the boat. Sometimes we go to the Rappahannock River, sometimes the Mattaponi River, but we only hunt snapping turtles. They have the most meat, and they don't eat from the bottom like other turtles do."

Turtle hunting, or trapping, is only done in the warmer months, July through October. When it gets cold the turtles stay in the warmer water at the bottom of the river, but when it's warm they like to sun themselves on trees or rocks. The hunt begins with a special ceremony. Assistant Chief Fortune says, "We ask the Great Creator for a good hunt, and we always give thanks for whatever we catch. That's something we have to do. That was the way I was brought up. A few other men and I pick a spot and walk around and look for turtles. You very rarely see a really big one sitting out there in the river, but if you see smaller ones sunning themselves, nine times out of ten you'll find bigger ones you don't see. That's where we set our traps. Our ancestors used small sapling trees, sharpened the ends, ran twine through a notch, and put bait, eel or cut up fish, on it. Nowadays some use metal poles, but I still use a sapling. The reason for the sharpened end is that you need to stab it into the dirt at the bottom of the river, and you need to stick it in pretty deep. You have to be careful and not put it too close to the bank, because if the turtle can get his claws into anything he can pull the whole thing out. So you want to put the trap in pretty deep water where he can't touch bottom, so he can't get a grip on anything to pull the pole out. After the traps are set, we check them twice a day, morning and evening.

"Once we've caught a turtle, we bring it home and put it in a barrel or tub of water and keep it there for seven days. We purify them by giving them just a little lettuce or cabbage to eat, no meat or anything like that. This purifies their system; it cleans their insides out. Before we kill the turtle we do another ceremony, a blessing for the turtle. That means something to us because he's giving his life for us. Once he's been killed we put him in scalding water for a few minutes. That loosens the skin from the shell so we can cut the shell off. Then we cut the meat out. Nothing is wasted, everything is used. Sometimes we use the shell for a shield."

Assistant Chief Fortune says the turtle meat can be fried or made into a stew. "Different people have different recipes. A lot of people make it into a stew. My mom would add water, potatoes, and corn, and cook it in a big iron pot over an open fire. We did this when my brother got married. A lot of people from Richmond who were friends of my brother and his wife came, and they sat around eating it, but they didn't know what it was. They probably wouldn't have tried it if they knew it was turtle stew, but after they learned what it was they said they really enjoyed it."

Other Indians who live in rural areas still hunt, fish and grow vegetables in small gardens for some of their diet. Those who live near tidal rivers like the Pamunkey and Mattaponi Rivers catch shad in the spring. The fish are heading up river to spawn, so many are full of eggs.

Ivy Bradley works at the Pamunkey Fish Hatchery where shad eggs are hatched, and the fry are fed until they are old enough to be released back into the Pamunkey River. This gives them a better chance of surviving than if they were born in the river. The eggs and sperm are collected from the fishing that is done in the

TURTLE STEW

SHAD

afternoon. But when the Pamunkey fishermen fish the other tides, they keep the fish and fish eggs, or roe, for their families to eat.

Ivy's wife, Kay, says shad has a wonderful taste, but a lot of people don't like it because it is so bony. She says that if you bake the fish for seven hours at 325 degrees the bones dissolve. But Ivy prefers the way she fixes the roe. She puts salt and pepper on it, then wraps bacon around the roe. Then she wraps waxed paper around the bundle of roe and bacon and folds the ends in to make a package. She cooks it for about fifteen minutes in a deep fryer. Wrapping it in the waxed paper keeps the eggs from popping. She says if you don't do that, the eggs will pop out and burn you. When the paper turns brown, the roe is done.

Virginia Indians cooked fish, especially shad, on

Cooking tip: bake shad for seven hours at 325 degrees to dissolve the bones.

SHAD PLANKING

wooden racks over the open fire (see the Theodore DeBry print above). That practice has evolved into a special political event which today ushers in the spring campaign season in Virginia — shad planking. Politicians gather to enjoy the fish that has been cooked on wooden planks for several hours over an open fire.

Like their ancestors, the Pamunkey Indians and other Virginia tribes also hunt deer and wild turkey. The Monacans, who lived in the far western part of the state, also hunted buffalo occasionally. They may have had to leave their territory to find buffalo, and it was not their main source of meat, but they did eat it occasionally.

Although she was a city girl, Mary Wade, a Monacan Indian, still fixed buffalo. Of course anyone who wants buffalo meat today has to buy it. Mary found it at a local grocery store, but usually got it from Georgetown Farm, which is twenty-five miles north of Charlottesville, Virginia. She felt it was actually healthier for people than beef because it contains 23 – 30% more protein than beef, and has half the fat content of beef.

Mary made buffalo stew using the meat the same way others use beef.

She also prepared roast buffalo. To cook it that way she poked a few holes in the roast and inserted crushed garlic. She then smeared the whole roast with garlic. After wrapping it in aluminum foil the roast was cooked slowly for six hours.

Today, most Indians merely supplement their diets with food they grow or hunt, but in the early days of Virginia, where you lived deter-

---

Mary Wade's Buffalo Stew

Brown Buffalo meat
Add:

 chopped onions
 sliced carrots
 quartered potatoes
 1 package of onion soup mix
 1 can of drained tomatoes
 chopped celery
 dash of Worcestershire sauce

Simmer for a least 2 hours. To thicken stew blend 2 tsp. of corn starch with 1/4 cup water and add to stew.

Marie "Drifting Moon" Adkins' Corn Pudding

2/3 cup of sugar
2 beaten eggs
1/2 stick of margarine
2 tablespoons corn starch
1 cup creamed corn
1 cup whole kernel corn
1 can evaporated milk

Mix the above ingredients well and pour into a two quart oven-proof casserole dish or 9"x 9" square pan. Bake in a 350 degree oven for approximately 1 hour.

We're Still Here

Debora "Littlewing" Moore's
Fry Bread

1/2 package of powdered milk
3 cups of unbleached flour
1 cup warm water
1/2 cup of whole milk
1 tablespoon baking powder
1 teaspoon salt

Use your hands to mix the above ingredients in a large bowl. You may have to add flour as you go if the dough gets too sticky. Mix until smooth. Do not over mix. Cover with a damp cloth. Let rest for at least 30 minutes up to 2 hours.

Pinch off an egg-sized amount and stretch it out. Make sure it's stretched thin, especially the edges because you don't want it to puff too much.

Put at least 1" of oil in a pan and heat until hot. The oil is ready when a piece of dough sizzles and instantly starts to brown. Gently and slowly lay the pieces of dough in the hot oil. Fry until dough is a light, golden brown. Drizzle with honey, or sprinkle with powdered sugar.

Debora also makes pizza with her fry bread by covering the cooked circles with mozzarella cheese and pizza sauce. She puts this in the oven until the cheese melts.

Debora explains that the first attempt at making fry bread may not be perfect. As she says, "There is an art to making fry bread, and it takes practice."

mined what you ate. Indians in the coastal area fished for sturgeon and herring and gathered shell fish like oysters, mussels, and clams. Indians living along streams and rivers in most parts of the state ate turtle, while deer and bear were mentioned by early English writers as the most important large animals that provided Indians with food.

The Algonquian-speaking tribes were part of a farming culture, and more than half of their diet each year came from vegetables grown in their fields. The writings of William Strachey, an English settler, tell us that each house had a garden that was 100 or 200 feet square. He also commented that it was the women and children who were the ones who cared for the fields, although it was the men who prepared the land for planting.

Fertile soil usually determined their village sites, and the Indians sometimes moved a village when the soil would no longer grow corn. Preparation for a new garden was done a year in advance. The men killed the trees by bruising the bark next to the roots and burning around the base to kill the roots. The following year they would dig up the ground. In open areas the men loosened the soil to a depth of a few inches, and then the women used a planting stick to make rows of holes in the ground approximately three feet apart. In those holes they planted four grains of corn and two seeds of beans. In the spaces between the holes squash or pumpkins were planted. Some still use this method of planting today because it works so well. The corn stalks provide support for the beans, and the squash leaves shade the roots of the corn and bean plants.

The settlers at Jamestown undoubtedly owed their lives to the Indians' ability to grow corn, and their generosity in sharing it in the early days of the settlement. Corn was basic to many recipes and eventually became an important trade item between the Indians and settlers. However, according to an interpreter at Jamestown Settlement, the settlers felt they were demeaned by having to eat corn since it was only used as pig feed back in England. Nevertheless they copied the Indian method of making simple corn cakes by mixing hot water with corn meal and frying them. The settlers fried their cakes in iron skillets, but the Indians fried theirs on a flat rock placed over or near an outdoor fire.

Corn was so important to one tribe, the Chickahominy, that it became part of their identity. They are known as "Coarse-ground Corn People." Mayflower Adkins, a Chickahominy Indian, grows corn and other vegetables on her farm in Charles City County, Virginia. She was raised on corn and now uses it for everything. She cooks hominy for breakfast and corn bread, corn cakes, and corn soup for lunch or dinner, plus corn custard and corn pudding for dessert. Fried corn kernels are used as a vegetable with a meal, or with sugar or honey for a dessert.

Her father used to make hominy in the winter. Mayflower doesn't know exactly how he did it, but remembers that he would take ashes from an oak wood

GARDENING

CORN

Fried corn kernels are used as a vegetable with a meal, or with sugar or honey for a dessert.

95

Mayflower Adkins, a Chickahominy Indian, grows corn and other vegetables on her farm in Charles City County, Virginia.

FRY BREAD

fire, put them in water in a big iron pot, and cook the corn in there. She says, "I buy hominy in the store now. For breakfast I fry up some bacon, then put the hominy in the pan, and cook it with the bacon on top. A friend of mine saw me do it that way once and asked where I got the recipe. I said, 'It's my own recipe, I made it up.' She said, 'I didn't know you could cook without a recipe.' I told her, 'Well, where do you think the first recipe came from? You try something and if it comes out good, you've got a recipe.'"

She used to hunt deer with her husband before he died. "I had to hunt. It was the only way I could see him in the winter." Her five children all hunted, even the four girls. She says, "When I'd pick some peas, I'd say, 'Sally, go get me a squirrel,' and she'd take the gun and come back with one. I like to cook squirrel with my peas. I've always done it that way."

Last year her six-year-old granddaughter, Tashina "White Dove" Holmes, helped her shuck and freeze her corn. They shucked it down to one or two layers of husk and then put it in freezer bags and into the freezer. She says that by freezing it that way it tastes like it's right out of the garden when you take it out and cook it.

Another favorite Indian food is fry bread. Originating out West, today you can find it all around the country, especially at pow wows. Fry bread is a light bread-like dough that is flattened into a circle and deep fried. It is served with honey, or as an Indian taco with ground beef, lettuce and shredded cheese.

In the old days much of the Indians' food was cooked over an outdoor fire rather than inside the yehakin. The methods they used, boiling in a clay pot, roasting on a spit, or frying on rocks are ones used today, except now they use different equipment and appliances. Actually, the Algonquian word for the outdoor kitchen is one that is widely used today — barbecue.

Virginia Indians helped domesticate many foods that now feed much of the world. Beans, potatoes, squash, sunflowers and corn are used as everything from vegetables to oils. And the favorite of many, chocolate, comes from the cocoa bean which was not grown in Virginia but was cultivated by New World Indians.

Chapter 11

Presenting Their Stories: NMAI, Jamestown and Beyond

It was a kaleidoscope of colors, textures, and even languages, as thousands of Native peoples gathered for the opening of the Smithsonian's National Museum of the America Indian on the Mall in Washington, D.C. in the spring of 2004. Two special events made up the Grand Opening ceremonies.

The day began with a Native Nations Procession, a walk from the Smithsonian Institution Building, often called the "Castle" along the National Mall toward the U. S. Capitol. This is thought to have been one of the largest gatherings of Native peoples in modern history. Warren Cook, a vice-chief of the Pamunkey Tribe participated in the

Allyn Cook

Left to right: W. Richard West, Jr., a citizen of the Cheyenne and Arapaho Tribes of Oklahoma and Founding Director of the Smithsonian's National Museum of the American Indian; Pamunkey Chief William Miles; and Austin Sky Alfonso at the opening ceremonies of the National Museum of the American Indian (2003).

walk, and then attended the opening dedication ceremony at the Museum. There he watched his granddaughter, Austin Star Alfonso, join Pamunkey Chief William Miles, and W. Richard West, Jr., a citizen of the Cheyenne and Arapaho Tribes of Oklahoma, a Peace Chief of the Southern Cheyenne, and the founding director of the National Museum of the American Indian, in the ceremony at the museum. With thousands of Indians in their traditional regalia, the ceremony was a colorful and emotional event. Leaders of the tribes and the youth of the tribes were honored. Indians were chosen to represent the four directions of the compass- north, south, east, and west for the ceremony. Vice-chief Cook's granddaughter Austin, and Chief Miles represented the east.

"We were honored to be represented in the opening ceremonies, but we are also proud to be included in one of the permanent exhibits in the museum," says Vice-chief Cook. The Pamunkey Tribe is part of the museum display titled "Our Lives" located on the third floor, which shows how several tribes live today.

Vice-chief Cook feels the Pamunkey Tribe was chosen to be featured in this section for several reasons. "We are one of the oldest reservations in the United States, and were one of the first tribes to make contact with the English. Our treaties actually pre-date the United States, because they were made with the King of England. Plus we still have our own tribal government. We never stopped governing ourselves. We still do it today as we did it 400 years ago, and we still continue some of the traditional things that we have done for hundreds of years. We still fish, and hunt, and make pottery with clay dug from the banks of the Pamunkey River. We have one of the oldest Indian churches in the state, and one of the oldest shad fish hatcheries in the United States. And we're still honoring the treaty we made with the English and pay our taxes, or our tribute, as we did to the colonial governor with a deer each fall. Except now we pay that tribute to the governor of the state of Virginia."

The NMAI showcases the lives and art of Native peoples of both North and South America, and is so large that many feel it takes more than one visit to see all the exhibits.

In Virginia there are many smaller museums that tell the story of one tribe or one region. For example, in Amherst County the people of the Monacan Nation have converted their old schoolhouse into a museum.

"We all went to school here. Three or four generations of the Monacan people went through grade seven in these buildings." Phyllis Hicks is talking about the three buildings that now form the Monacan Museum in Amherst County. As the museum director, she knows its history well, "My mother and I went to school here. In my mother's time there were just two buildings, and she could only go through the seventh grade. Then they added a cinder block building for the eighth grade. I went through the eighth grade, and then they integrated the schools, so I went to Amherst High School."

Because of the period of racial discrimination that all Indians in Virginia went through, some Monacan Indians moved away from the area, or hid their Indian identity. Many are now returning to their tribal roots, but some of the children have not had the benefit of years of learning about their tribe from the elders of the tribe. "We started out trying to educate our own children. We wanted them to know who they are, and to be proud of who they are. We wanted to teach them about the Monacans." Phyllis says.

It took several years to get the money to convert the old school buildings into a museum. Work began in 1995 with a new roof, new walls with insulation, and new lighting. Then everything had to be painted. In October,

MONACAN MUSEUM

1998 the three room museum opened.

Now one room houses a collection of artifacts including arrowheads, pottery, and woven baskets. Some of the baskets on display are woven with honeysuckle vines, which is the traditional Monacan method of making baskets. Phyllis remembers her great-grandmother making honeysuckle baskets, "I wish I had learned how to do it from her. But I was young, and you know how it is, I didn't have time, I was too busy playing and doing other things. But there are two ladies making that type of basket now, and we make gift sets with them. We put our jellies and jams in them, and sell them here to raise money for the museum and other projects."

Another room contains a video library. One video was made by Monacan Indians about their tribe, and others are about Indian history in general. Monacans differ from other state recognized Virginia tribes in that they were not part of the Powhatan group, and did not speak an Algonquin based language. They probably spoke a language related to Eastern Siouan tribes, and are closely related to the Occaneechi and Saponi tribes. Because of their location in the Piedmont region of Virginia, they had access to copper. This metal was highly prized by all Indians. The Monacans mined copper and became proficient traders with other Indian tribes.

The third room at their museum is used as a research office where people can trace their Monacan roots. Tribal members also use this area to work on documentation for projects like the attempt for federal recognition.

Other tribes including the Nansemond, Pamunkey, and Mattaponi have their own museums. Other tribes have hopes of opening museums to tell their own story.

Almost all of the museums that depict the history of an area in Virginia start with a display about Indian

OTHER INDIAN MUSEUMS

life. A few examples are:

- THE OCCANEECHI STATE PARK VISITOR CENTER in Clarksville (804) 374-2210
- THE VIRGINIA MUSEUM OF NATURAL HISTORY in Martinsville (540) 666-8634
- FLOWERDUE HUNDRED in Prince George County (804) 541-8938
- THE CHESTERFIELD HISTORICAL SOCIETY AND MUSEUMS in Chesterfield County (804) 777-9663
- MACCALLUM MORE MUSEUM AND GARDENS in Chase City (804) 372-0502

See Resources section for additional listings of museums and living history sites.

The Pamunkey Indian Museum on the reservation. The arch of the roof echoes the arch of their historic houses.

The Valentine Museum in Richmond even has a box of arrowheads that they credit with being the beginning of the museum. Mann Valentine's fascination with the arrowheads he found prompted him to start the collections that were the foundation for the museum.

The Virginia Historical Society in Richmond is home to one of the most comprehensive museum displays. The first two galleries of the permanent exhibit

"The Story of Virginia" are devoted to Indian artifacts from Prehistoric times to the Contact Period. Panels also explain how Indians made and used their tools, and what their life was like.

Some museums, like the Wolf Creek Indian Village and Museum in Bastian, Virginia, feature costumed guides and a reconstructed Indian village. Owned and operated by the Bland County Historical Society it is based on information gained from a nearby archaeological site which dates to circa 1215. In 1997 construction began on a museum to hold artifacts excavated from the village site, as well as from sites throughout the southwestern Virginia region.

There is also a small reconstructed Powhatan village at the 1611 Citie of Henricus in Chesterfield County located near Dutch Gap. And members of the Monacan Nation are presenting interpretive programs as they build the Monacan Indian Village at Natural Bridge in the Shenandoah Valley.

Shirley "Little Dove" Custalow McGowan, a Mattaponi Indian, creates a living history museum wherever she and her son Samuel "Opechancanough" present their programs on Pocahontas' People. They travel to schools, community organizations, museums, historical sites and pow wows. Dressed in traditional dress, they use artifacts to demonstrate the skills of their ancestors. They often construct a small village setting with a hunting and fishing encampment to take visitors back through time to learn the true history of the Powhatan Indian people. Food demonstrations may include cooking over an open fire, and methods of preserving food such as drying corn, beans, and squash, and smoking fish and red meat on wooden smoking racks. Exhibits of clothing, bows and arrows, fire making tools, stone tooling, bone tooling, drills and cordage are also available for viewers to examine. Little Dove states that her programs teach the importance of respect and honor of one's self, other people and the natural environment; values that have been passed down from her ancestors.

Jamestown-Yorktown Foundation

The recreated Powhatan Indian Village at Jamestown Settlement.

A larger Powhatan village has been recreated at Jamestown Settlement. Children visiting this living history museum are often surprised to hear an interpreter in Indian attire ask them if they would like to be a scarecrow. But it's not really such a strange question as gardens in villages of tribes of the Powhatan group were guarded by living scarecrows. These were usually young children who sat in a little hut on a platform in the garden, and threw rocks or sticks to keep crows or animals from eating the plants.

At Jamestown Settlement visitors can see the type of hut one would have found in a garden, as well the type of houses the Indians lived in. Occasionally visitors will find an interpreter sewing together mats woven from bull rushes to be used as the walls and roof of a scarecrow hut or house.

JAMESTOWN SETTLEMENT

HISTORIC JAMESTOWNE

Visitors might also watch interpreters demonstrating cooking over an open hearth, weaving a gathering basket, making a rack for drying and smoking foods, or tanning a deer hide.

With many of the same tools and techniques that the Indians employed, the costumed staff members demonstrate ways the Powhatan Indians used the natural environment to provide them with the necessities of life. The demonstrations change according to the seasons to reflect the tasks that the Indians would have been performing at that particular time of year.

In addition to museum galleries there is also a recreated fort with costumed interpreters showing the lifestyle of the settlers who interacted with the Powhatan Indians in the area, as well as re-creations of the "Susan Constant", the "Godspeed" and the "Discovery" – the three ships that brought the first settlers, 104 men and boys, to Virginia.

Starting in 1807 and every fifty years since there has been a commemoration of the founding of Jamestown. Today, the island site of the original town is formally known as Historic Jamestowne and it is co-administered by the National Park Service and the Association for the Preservation of Virginia Antiquities (APVA). However, the actual observance has not always been held on Jamestown Island. One of the largest observances occurred in 1907 for Jamestown's Ter-Centennial anniversary. This major exposition was constructed on the site that today is the Norfolk Naval Base. Interestingly, the U.S. Navy is still using some of the original buildings from the 1907 Jamestown Exposition. President Theodore Roosevelt spoke at the opening ceremony in 1907 and the seven-month exposition drew 1.2 million visitors to Norfolk. This was the era of the Wild West Show featuring cowboys and Indians parading in full regalia and dramatizing battles from the Plains Indian Wars as well roping, riding and other rodeo events. The 1907 Jamestown Exposition featured the 101 Ranch from Oklahoma, which was one of the biggest traveling Wild West Shows of the day. While most of the Indians seen by visitors to the 1907 exposition were from the American West, Virginia Indians were represented in Norfolk. Men and women of the Pamunkey Tribe performed in a play about two of Virginia's most famous Native people, Pocahontas and her father Chief Powhatan. The play featured a dramatization of the rescue of Captain John Smith by the young Pocahontas, and was very popular with visitors.

In 1957, the 350th commemoration focused on Virginia's Historic Triangle and involved several important organizations; the Commonwealth of Virginia, the Association for the Preservation of Virginia Antiquities, the National Park Service, The Colonial Williamsburg Foundation, The College of William & Mary, as well as state and federal commissions. This event saw the cre-

Jamestown-Yorktown Foundation

The new theater and special exhibition building at Jamestown Settlement.

ation of the Jamestown Festival Park, now known as Jamestown Settlement as well as the completion of the Colonial Parkway from Williamsburg to Jamestown. However, the highlight of the 1957 event was a visit from Britain's Queen Elizabeth II and Prince Phillip in October of 1957. The Festival Park included two living history areas; one a recreation of a Powhatan Indian village and the other a recreation of the English fort. For the first time members from the Virginia Indian community worked as interpreters of Powhatan culture. Doris and Jim Ware and several other members of the Rappahannock Tribe demonstrated basket making, hide tanning, house construction, canoe building as well as food preparation. Just like 1907 the 1957 commemoration highlighted the life of Pocahontas. However, this time

James and Doris Ware, Rappahannock Indians, at the Jamestown Festival Park, 1950s.

Presenting Their Stories: NMAI, Jamestown and Beyond

Si Waugaman

Colonial Williamsburg Visitor's Center — The Regional Visitor's Center for Jamestown 2007.

instead of a play about her rescue of John Smith the marriage of Pocahontas and John Rolfe was reenacted on Jamestown Island. Memorabilia from the 1907 and 1907 remain popular among collectors.

Planning to commemorate the 400th anniversary began in 1997. Members of the Virginia Council on Indians and tribal leaders served on several organizing committees and the federal commission. This time Virginia Indians are seeking a more comprehensive discussion of Colonial history — one that emphasizes that Native peoples lived in the region for thousands of years before the arrival of European settlers in the proposed museum exhibits at Historic Jamestown and Jamestowne Settlement. Representatives from the tribes have reviewed the text for the exhibit panels that deal with Virginia Indian history and culture as well as the scripts for film clips at the planned exhibits.

We're Still Here

Once again the event for 2007 is focusing on the Historic Triangle; Jamestown, Williamsburg and Yorktown. Organizers feel that these three locations represent three major phases in the beginning of what has become the United States of America. Jamestown was the first permanent English settlement and the first capitol, Williamsburg the second capital of the colony and where the ideas that led to the Revolution were born, and Yorktown is the site where the Revolutionary War was won. These three places complete the circle of the formation of our nation just as they form a circular route visitors can take in the Tidewater area of Virginia for the 2007 commemoration.

However, this commemoration will speak to the complexities of Powhatan society in 1607 as well as letting visitors know that Virginia Indians are still here!

Chapter 12

Reflections

"Even during his last hours of life he asked for daily reports on the progress of federal recognition." Chief Anne Richardson was remembering the strength and guidance that her father, the late Chief Emeritus Captain O. Nelson, gave to the Rappahannock Tribe throughout his lifetime. Under his leadership the Rappahannock Tribe gained state recognition and he worked to secure the future of his people until the time of his passing. Chief Emeritus Nelson was not the only Virginia Indian leader to "walk on" during the spring of 2003.

During a span on four weeks the Virginia Indian community lost four prominent members of the community; three tribal chiefs and the president of VITAL (Virginia Indian Tribal Alliance for Life). The deaths of Chief Captain Nelson of the Rappahannock Tribe, Chief Daniel Webster "Little Eagle" Custalow of the Mattaponi Tribe — both on the same day. It was March 21st and the first day of Spring. The following Friday, Chief Emeritus Tecumseh "Deerfoot" Cook of the Pamunkey Tribe died. Three Fridays later Mary "Laughing Dove" Wade of VITAL and a member of the Monacan Indian Nation died. It was an extraordinarily difficult time for the Virginia Indian community. Each of the chiefs served in the official leadership capacities for more than 30 years and Mary Wade worked tirelessly for the Virginia Indian community for much of the last decade. Thus the combined number of years given to their respective tribal communities by these special individuals totaled more than a century. The chiefs in particular held their people together during difficult times of the twentieth century. Each of the four individuals helped to bring the eight state-recognized tribes into the twenty-first century. That their lifetimes overlapped was seen as a blessing by many in the native community.

Chief Webster "Little Eagle" Custalow was born on the Mattaponi Indian Reservation in 1912 and lived there until his death. Chief Webster was noted for his ability to tell stories that highlighted life on the Mattaponi Reservation and emphasized community values. Sharing stories set in the 1930s during the Depression, Chief Webster told of the hardships faced by his tribe during those difficult years. Chief Webster's reminiscences of sharing groceries with families in need both on and off the reservation and of hunting while a young boy for turkeys and quail to be used for tribute payment were charming but also always taught a lesson. One story in particular told of the time he went hunting as a youngster. Little Eagle shot two turkeys and brought them home to his father expecting to be praised. Rather than getting praise for his ability as a hunter, the young Little Eagle was punished for shooting two turkeys instead of one. By shooting two turkeys Little Eagle had taken more food than his father thought was necessary. He always remembered that lesson and tried hard to share the concept of taking care of the environment.

During his last years as chief of the Mattaponi, Webster "Little Eagle" Custalow fought against efforts to dam the Cohoke Creek, a tributary of the Mattaponi River. Growing up and living on that Mattaponi Reservation, which sits along the bank of the Mattaponi River, taught Chief Webster the necessity of protecting the river since his tribe has fished the river for centuries drawing sustenance from its beautiful waters. Chief Webster's life exemplified the personal qualities that are most valued in the role of chief. Chief Webster Custalow's eldest son, Dr. Linwood "Little Bear" Custalow, summaries the qualities of his father, "My father was a hard worker. He always shared what he had. It didn't have to be someone on the reservation. He was a straightforward, honest guy; a guy you could slap on one cheek and he would turn the other. If you asked him to go one mile, he would go the second. That is the type of person he was. He was a big respecter of the environment. He not only fought for the Mattaponi River but for the eagles. He was a fighter for the rights of things." Chief Webster is remembered for many things; his strong Christian faith, the love for his family and tribe and his efforts to protect the Mattaponi River. Carl "Lone Eagle" Custalow, following in the footsteps of his late father is now the Mattaponi Chief and plans to draw on the example of leadership shown to him by his father.

Not far from the Mattaponi Reservation lies the Pamunkey Reservation; the home of the late Chief Cook. Debora Moore of the Pamunkey Indian Women's Circle notes that Chief Cook was known as "Peach" to his close family and fellow tribal members; Peach was a nickname Tecumseh got from his mother. When she saw Tecumseh she would say to him "Come give me my peaches!" "Peaches meant kisses, so he was called Peach," remembers Debora.

Chief Cook was 103 years of age when he died, and hunted and fished well into his 90s. At his funeral mourners were reminded that Chief Cook was born in 1899 and lived in three centuries and during the terms of 19 U.S. presidents. For most of his life he was in good

We're Still Here

health and made every attempt to participate in the cultural life of his tribe. Even in his last years Chief Cook would play a small hand-held drum at the annual payment of tribute in November at the capitol in Richmond. "When Peach would wear his regalia and bring out his drum, it would bring many to tears the way he smiled and held his face upward to the heavens. Watching him dance felt like we were watching our ancestors dance. No one dances like they did anymore. He would give his war cry and send chills throughout the crowd. He danced at his 100th birthday party! He had a great sense of humor and was always telling stories of the old days. I know he was very proud of being an Indian man. His memory will live on forever with our people."

Each of the three chiefs were men of strong Christian faith and like their fellow tribesmen they worked hard to support their families. Being chief does not pay a salary and gainful employment on the reservations or in rural Virginia is not easily found. Chief Tecumseh Cook worked as a hunting guide and Chief Webster worked in the lumber industry. Chief Nelson was employed as an interpreter and educator of traditional Virginia Indian lifeways at Jamestown Festival

Webster "Little Eagle" Custalow, Chief of theMattaponi (2001).

Park (the precursor to Jamestown Settlement in Williamsburg). It was there, in 1957, that Chief Nelson met a young Queen Elizabeth visiting Jamestown for the

350th anniversary of the English settlement.

When asked to reflect on the significance of the lives and leadership of her father and the two late chiefs, Chief Anne Richardson of the Rappahannock Tribe said, "To me, my Dad was larger than life... I had so much respect for these men. They were like warriors who had sacrificed it all for their people. They instilled in us examples of personal sacrifice which gave us strength to believe in and work for a better tomorrow for our people. Although they were all very quiet beings, they were above all the most loving and compassionate people I have ever met. Like anchors they were grounded so deep in our culture. I saw these men as living legends of strength, knowledge, wisdom and power."

The loss of Mary Wade in any given year would have been a terrible blow to the Monacan Indian Nation and the Virginia Indian community as a whole. However, coming so soon after the death of three prominent chiefs was particularly difficult. A former member of the Virginia Council on Indians, Mary Wade worked closely with the late Thomasina E. Jordan on everything from pow wows to establishing the political action group known as VITAL or the Virginia Indian Tribal Alliance for Life. A woman with a heart of gold and a ready smile, Mary brought energy and dedication to everything she did. Mary spearheaded the legislative drive for federal recognition for six of Virginia's tribes. Mary helped to create policy for VITAL and worked hard organizing fund raising activities for the federal recognition effort. With Mary's help, six Virginia tribes began the quest for federal recognition in 2000. In September of 2002, sub-committee hearings were held in the U.S. House of Representatives and in October of that same year testimony in favor of federal recognition was presented to the U.S.

Senate Committee on Indian Affairs. In May of 2003, Congressman James P. Moran (D-VA) and Congresswoman Jo Ann Davis (R-VA) introduced the Thomasina E. Jordan Virginia Indian Federal Recognition Bill (H.R. 1938) in the U.S. House of Representatives. Senator George Allen (R-VA) introduced the bill in the U.S. Senate.

As of 2006, action is still pending on this legislation. Whatever the outcome much of the current status of the federal recognition effort may be attributed to Mary's initial efforts in establishing VITAL.

Remembering Mary Wade fondly, Debora Moore remarked, "Mary was the glue that held our tribes together. To me she was like a paramount chief. She spent her days to the end doing what she felt she could for the Virginia Indians. Mary never complained about being tired, never spoke harsh words about anyone and she never gave up. Mary always extended a helping hand to anyone who needed it. It is still hard to believe that she will not physically be present at the pow wows or meetings, but it is a relief to know that her spirit is always with us. Mary is right here walking and dancing beside us."

Today, new members to the Virginia Council on Indians take their seats each month to work in conjunction with the current chiefs and other tribal organizations to support the goals of Virginia's first people. It is not possible to replace those special people from the Virginia Indian community who have "walked on" but their example of dedication and leadership will show a new generation of native leaders what the late Thomasina E. Jordan called "the indelible thread of red." That thread of red marks the pathway of tradition and service toward a better future for Virginia Indians.

Educators:

Suggested uses for this book in the classroom.

We are pleased to note that classroom educators have found this book helpful in presenting Native people in a contemporary setting as well as meeting their lesson objectives. The subject matter in this book supports Virginia SOLs 2.2, 2.4, VS.2d, VS.2e, VS.3g, VS.4b, USI.3b, and USI.4b. *We're Still Here* stresses the continuity of today's Virginia tribes with their past. Over and over the authors were told that this is one of the most important points to make to students, parents and teachers. We tried to do so by including the voices and personal stories of Virginia's Native people.

Keeping this in mind, ask students to reflect upon the role of history in Virginia Indian identity. After reading Chapter 1 ask students to discuss aspects of life on the Mattaponi or Pamunkey Reservation and the relationship that treaties have to the establishment of the reservations. A treaty is a formal agreement between two or more sovereign nations. Virginia has two of the oldest reservations in the country. Therefore what is the importance of these reservations to Virginia's indigenous people? What kinds of rights did the Treaty of 1677 guarantee to the tribes?

Use other chapters to identify the names and responsibilities of leaders in the Native community. What are some of the main issues facing Virginia's tribes at this time? How are the tribes working with state agencies, universities and other organizations to address some of these issues?

Working with primary documents is an important skill to develop with students. Ask students to compare the John Smith map of 1612 (shown on page 22) with the map on page 24, indicating the current tribal locations of the eight state-recognized tribes. What is the relationship between these two documents? Ask students to name the eight state-recognized tribes. Encourage students to attend a pow wow. Use the suggested resources in this book to learn more about Virginia Indians!

Glossary

Algonquian— A major linguistic grouping of languages with similar grammatical patterns and vocabulary. Algonquian languages were spoken by numerous tribes of the Northeastern part of North America, tribes along the Great Lakes, and even on the Great Plains. The Powhatans spoke an Algonquian language, but it is now extinct. However, other Algonquian-speaking tribes have retained their languages, such as the Ojibwa and the Cheyenne.

artifact—An object made, used or modified by human beings.

Chief Emeritus— An honorary title of address for a former chief or leader.

Contact, pre-Contact, post-Contact — Time periods and the interaction between native populations and non-native settlers. Generally, these terms are used to talk about the time periods associated with the European settlement of North and South America, beginning in the late 15th century. It is during this era that "contact" was ongoing and sustained into the present era. Pre-contact may be substituted for the term pre-historic. Post-contact implies continuous interaction and settlement in the area by non-indigenous people.

cultural patrimony — Objects that hold great significance for a particular group and may be linked to their identity. Objects of cultural patrimony may not be owned by any individual but are the property of the group as a whole.

DeBry, Theodore — (also Theodor de Bry) Theodore DeBry is best known for his documentation of early expeditions to the Americas. DeBry was a goldsmith, engraver, print and book-seller in Frankfurt, Germany. From 1590 until his death in 1598, DeBry produced several volumes depicting early life in the Americas. Each volume included graphic illustrations often made from first-hand observations. His family finished several of his works and continued production until 1634.

demographic collapse —The rapid decline in the total population of a specific group. American Indians experienced widespread demographic collapse with the introduction of European diseases during the colonial encounter.

extant — Still existing or remaining, not extinct.

hierarchical — A term that indicates the existence of a system in which groups, persons or objects are arranged or ordered by rank.

horticulturists — A term used to denote the growing of crops for food without the use of the plow. Virginia Indians were horticulturists and cultivated extensive gardens. However, they used digging sticks not plows to plant their gardens.

indigenous — A term used to refer to the native or original inhabitants of a specific location. "Native American" is a more recent term used to denote the indigenous inhabitants of North America. Many of Virginia's indigenous population are not comfortable with the term Native American. They feel that anyone born in the United States is a native American. The term "American Indian" has a longer history of usage, but like the term Native American it is problematic. The European explorers called the native peoples they initially encountered Indians since they thought they had arrived on islands off Asia. Most native people prefer to be identified by their tribal names. Others would like to be called "First Americans," "First People" or "First Nations." (In this book the authors have used all three terms, but have used American Indians or Virginia Indians most frequently at the request of most of their interviewees.)

monolithic — A single unified way of being or construction.

pot sherds — Broken pieces of ceramics, usually found at archaeological sites. Pot sherds and ceramics preserve well in the archaeological record.

Powhatan —The term for the leader of a large chiefdom of Alkonquian-speaking people in the area of present-day Tidewater Virginia and parts of the Eastern Shore.

Racial Integrity Law of 1924 — Legislation adopted in Virginia and promoted by people who believed that the human race could be improved by applying the techniques of animal husbandry to humans. Such ideas were part of the Eugenics movement that attempted to stop the intermarrying and interbreeding of persons of different races. Proponents of the Eugenics movement were racial purists who sought to keep all races separate from one another. Among other things, the Racial Integrity Law outlawed marriage between persons of different races and declared that Virginia did not have any American Indians living in the Commonwealth. According to the Racial Integrity Law, persons were either white or colored. There was no category for Virginia Indians and they were to be classified as colored persons not Indians. The Racial Integrity Law was struck down by the U.S. Supreme Court in 1968.

Glossary

regalia — The proper term for American Indian cultural or ritual clothing. Regalia is highly individualistic and is assembled over a period of many years.

repatriation — To American Indians this term refers to the return or restoration of objects or human remains to their tribes of origin. In 1990 the U.S. adopted legislation mandating that federally-recognized tribes be notified by museums and other institutions of the holdings of human remains, funerary objects, sacred remains and objects of cultural patrimony that may be associated with the respective tribes. The law provides for the repatriation of these classes of objects to the federally-recognized tribes. This legislation is called the Native American Graves Protection and Repatriation Act or NAGPRA.

reservation — Land set aside for the use and benefit of an American Indian tribe by treaty or other formal agreement.

riverine — The environment in and around a river. This includes the land along the banks of the river and the resources associated with this environment.

subsistence — A term used to describe the fishing, hunting, gathering or agricultural practices of a group of people. Subsistence includes the practices, technology and strategies employed by people to successfully exist in their environment with the resources at-hand.

Tsenacommacah — A Powhatan word for the territory under the influence of the Powhatan Chiefdom. This territory included land east of the fall line of the Potomac, Rappahannock, York and James Rivers, and part of the Eastern Shore.

vestigial — Remaining original elements.

weir —A trap set in a stream or waterway for catching fish.

yehakin — The Powhatan word for house. Yehakins were made of woven mats sewn together over bent saplings. Archaeological excavations suggest that yehakins were built to accommodate single families.

Suggested Reading

Clash of Cultures: Prehistory – 1638
    by Christopher Collier and James Lincoln Collier
    Benchmark Books (1998)

Commoners, Tribute, and Chiefs: The Development of Algonkian
Culture in the Potomac Valley
    by Stephen R. Potter
    University of Virginia Press, Charlottesville (1993)

The Double Life of Pocahontas
    by Jean Fritz
    Grey Castle Press (1991)

First People: The Early Indians of Virginia
    by Keith Egloff and Deborah Woodward
    University Press of Virginia, Charlottesville, Virginia (1992)

Indian Island in Amherst County
    by Peter W. Houck
    Lynchburg Historical Research Company
    Lynchburg, Virginia (1984)

Pocahontas's People: The Powhatan Indians
of Virginia Through Four Centuries
    by Helen Rountree
    University of Oklahoma Press, Norman (1989)

We're Still Here

The Powhatan Indians of Virginia: Their Traditional Culture
    by Helen Rountree
    University of Oklahoma Press, Norman (1990)

The Powhatan Tribes
    by Christian Feest
    Chelsea House Publishers, New York (1990)

Powhatan's World and Colonial Virginia: A Conflict of Cultures
    by Frederic W. Gleach
    University of Nebraska Press (1997)

Virginia Indians: An Educational Coloring Book
    by the Virginia Museum of Natural History
    Martinsville, Virginia (1991)

Young Pocahontas in the Indian World
    by Helen Rountree.
    J & R Graphics Services
    Yorktown, Virginia (1995)

Brochures/Flyers

The Monacan Indians: Our Story
    by Karenne Wood and Diane Shields.
    The Monacan Indian Nation
    P.O. Box 1136
    Madison Heights, VA 24572

Pathways (Cultural events listing including local pow wows)
    Pepper Bird Foundation
    Available at Virginia Tourism Welcome Centers or
    Pepper Bird Foundation
    P.O. Box 1071
    Williamsburg, VA 23187 (include SASE)

Other Resources

Selected Websites:

www.wm.edu/airc
The American Indian Resource Center at the College of William &
Mary

www.powhatan.wm.edu
Information about the Werowocomoco archaeological site

www.Indians.vipnet.org
The Virginia Council on Indians and links to the 8 state-recognized
tribes

www.vitlva.org
Virginia Indian Tribal Alliance for Life (VITAL)

www.historyisfun.org
Jamestown-Yorktown Foundation, Jamestown Settlement

www.HistoricJamestown.org
The National Park Service and AVPA Preservation Virginia

www.apva.org
Association for the Preservation of Virginia Antiquities

www.vmnh.org
Virginia Museum of Natural History

www.caox.net/people/lwf/pepbird.htm
The Pepperbird Foundation

Videos

In Our Own Words: Voices of Virginia Indians.
Produced and directed by Danielle Moretti-Langholtz. 37-
minute award-winning documentary on Virginia's Eight State-
Recognized Tribes and an interactive CD-ROM.
www.wm.edu/airc

Reclaiming Our Heritage.
Produced and directed by Sharon Bryant, Monacan Indian
Nation, P.O. Box 1136, Madison Heights, VA 24572.

We're Still Here

Living History Museums:

Some of the museums such as Jamestown Settlement have living history interpreters in addition to their displays. The 1611 Citie of Henricus in Chesterfield County, (804) 706-1340, has a palisaded Native American village with interpreters, but no museum.

While the Monacan Indian Village at Natural Bridge in the Shenandoah Valley is being built, interpretive programs are being constructed on site about the Monacan building tools and methods, (804) 533-1410.

Museums: (see Chapter 11 for additional listings & information)

HISTORIC CRAB ORCHARD MUSEUM
& PIONEER PARK
Rt. 1, P.O. Box 194
Tazewell, VA 24651
(540) 988-6755

HISTORIC JAMESTOWNE
Colonial Parkway
(757) 898-2410

JAMESTOWN SETTLEMENT
P.O. Box 1607
Williamsburg, VA 23187
(757) 229-1607

MACCALLUM MORE MUSEUM
& GARDENS
603 Hudgin Street
Chase, VA 23924
(804) 372-0502

PAUMUNKEY INDIAN MUSEUM
Rt. 1, Box 2050
King William, VA 24019
(804) 843-4792

SMITHSONIAN NATIONAL MUSEUM
OF THE AMERICAN INDIAN
On the National Mall
Fourth Street & Independence Ave.,
S.W. Washington, DC 20560
(202) 633-1000

VIRGINIA'S EXPLORER PARK
P.O. Box 8508
Roanoke, VA 24014-0508
(540) 427-1800

VIRGINIA HISTORICAL SOCIETY
P.O. Box 7311
Richmond, VA 23221
(804) 358-4901

VIRGINIA MARINE SCIENCE MUSEUM
717 General Booth Boulevard
Virginia Beach, VA 23451
(757) 437-4949

VIRGINIA MUSEUM OF NATURAL
HISTORY
1001 Douglas Avenue
Martinsville, VA 24112
(540) 666-8634

WOLF CREEK INDIAN VILLAGE
& MUSEUM
Rt. 1, Box 1530
Bastian, VA 24314
(540) 688-3438

Eight State-Recognized Tribes of Virginia

(Used with permission of the Virginia Council on Indians.)

CHICKAHOMINY TRIBE
"Coarse Ground Corn People"
Providence Forge, Virginia
Chief: Stephen R. Adkins
State Recognized February 25, 1983

The Chickahominy Indian Tribe is located in Charles City County between Richmond and Williamsburg. Some tribal members live in communities in other parts of the state. The tribe is governed by a board of directors consisting of both male and female members. The tribe values strong religious beliefs: community and civic involvement, the pursuit of higher education, and pride in America. It considers all of these as necessary ingredients in maintaining the health, growth, and unity of the tribe. The population is approximately 1,000 persons.

EASTERN CHICKAHOMINY TRIBE
"Coarse Ground Corn People"
Providence Forge, Virginia
Chief: Marvin Bradby
State Recognized February 25, 1983

The Chickahominy Indians, Eastern Division, are located in New Kent County approximately twenty-five miles east of Richmond, Virginia. They are a small group organized for religious, educational, and benevolent reasons. The tribe, incorporated as a non-taxable organization to serve the needs of the community, is supported through contributions and dues-paying members. The population is approximately 150 persons.

MATTAPONI TRIBE
Mattaponi Indian Reservation
West Point, Virginia
Chief: Carl "Lone Eagle" Custalow
State Recognized February 25, 1983

The members of this tribe live on a reservation that stretches along the borders of the Mattaponi River in King William County, Virginia. Presently they number about seventy-five. Many of the younger members have left the reservation to seek work elsewhere. The Mattaponi Indian Reservation dates back to 1658. In those early days, the people made their living completely from nature's sources. Before the first settlers reached this land, these Indians served and worshiped the Great Spirit, who was their God in the Heavens above the sun, the moon, and the stars. Now they worship as Southern Baptists, and have their own church on the reservation. In 1646, the Mattaponi Indians began paying tribute to an early Virginia governor, and this custom continues to the present day when at Thanksgiving they present game or fish to the Governor of the Commonwealth of Virginia.

MONACAN NATION
Madison Heights, Virginia
Chief: Kenneth Branham
State Recognized February 14, 1989

Bear Mountain in Amherst County has been the home of the Monacan people for more than 10,000 years. Artifacts from hundreds of local archaeological sites reveal that during this time, Indian people thrived by gathering and hunting the area's rich natural resources. The earliest written histories of Virginia record that in 1607, the James River Monacans (along with their Manahoac allies on the Rappahannock River) controlled the area between the Fall Line in Richmond and the Blue Ridge Mountains. The most western of Virginia's eight recognized tribes, the Monacans were not part of the Powhatan Empire. They bring together the Siouan language and culture. The Monacans, over 700 strong, are currently involved in preserving their past heritage and ancient customs. St. Paul's Mission on Bear Mountain was chosen as the site for a Museum and Cultural Center due to open later this year. In presenting a deed of gift on October 7, 1995 to the Monacan Chief Kenneth Branham, Bishop Heath Light of the Episcopal Diocese ended nearly a century of church control over a small tract of Bear Mountain land that the Monacans hold sacred. While this gift involved only a 7-acre tract bordering the mission church founded in 1908, the property has always been considered the spiritual nexus of Monacan efforts to reestablish their identity. The tribe is working to regain the summit of Bear Mountain, with a plan for regrowth and agricultural management. They have begun a cultural

education program for the tribal members and a tribal
scholarship fund. They hold an annual homecoming
and bazaar the first Saturday in October at Bear Mountain. The Monacans today actively work to reclaim their
heritage.

NANSEMOND TRIBE
Chesapeake, Virginia
Chief: Barry W. Bass
State Recognized February 20, 1985

At the time of the Jamestown Settlement in 1607, the
Nansemond Tribe was located in the general area of
Reids Ferry, near Chuckatuck, in the current city of
Suffolk. Their "king" lived near Dumpling Island where
he kept his treasure houses. At that time,the tribe had a
population of approximately 1,200 persons with 300
bowmen. The early settlers raided the Nansemond
granaries and began the open hostilities between the
two communities. As increasing numbers of settlers
poured into the Nansemond River area, the tribal members relocated their reservation and tribal lands on several different occasions. The last 300 acres located on
the Nottaway River in Southampton County were sold
in 1791/1792. The tribe holds their monthly meetings at
the Indian United Methodist Church, which was
founded in 1850 as a mission for the Nansemond
Indians. The tribe is one of the remaining tribal groups
of the Powhatan Confederacy and has a population of
approximately 300 members.

PAMUNKEY TRIBE
King William, Virginia
Chief: "Swift Waters" Miles
State Recognized February 25, 1983

The Pamunkey Indians were the most powerful of the
tribes in the great Powhatan Confederacy which con-
sisted of approximately 32 to 34 tribes with some
10,000 people under the leadership of Chief Powhatan.
His territory encompassed the entire coastal plain from
the North Carolina border area to Washington D.C. The
Chief and his famous daughter Pocahontas lived
among the Pamunkey. The Pamunkey are exceedingly
proud of their history and enjoy telling how bravely their
ancestors resisted the encroachment of the white settlers. The Pamunkeys have the distinction of being one
of the tribes east of the Mississippi who have practiced

the art of pottery-making continuously since aboriginal times. The tribe of approximately 100 persons is located on the King William County Pamunkey Indian Reservation near Lester Manor, Virginia.

RAPPAHANNOCK TRIBE
"Where the Tide Ebbs and Flows"
Indian Neck, Virginia
Chief: G. Anne Richardson
State Recognized February 25, 1983

At the time of first contact with the English in 1607, their King's house, (Chief Kekataugh) and reservation occupied the Rappahannock River and much of Richmond County. The first of three treaties was signed in 1608 between the Rappahannocks and the colonial government. It established boundaries for their reservation. After many years of fighting to preserve their reservation lands, the Rappahannocks were moved by the 1670s to the present Tappahannock, Virginia location by order of the colonial government. Through many moves and struggles, the Rappahannocks' last reservation, which encompassed boundaries in Essex, King and Queen, and Caroline counties, was established by the Treaty of the Middle Plantation in 1677. This treaty identified the Rappahannocks as tributaries of Pamunkey. The present-day Rappahannocks live on much of these same lands even though they had lost their official reservation lands by the early 1700s. They still maintain a tribal government and headquarters which are located in Indian Neck, King & Queen County, Virginia. Today the tribe owns 21 acres of land in Indian Neck on which they have initiated a construction project to erect a three-phase cultural center complex. Phase one was completed in 1995. The second phase structure houses the civic center, providing space for live performances and exhibitions. The third phase will be a museum and archives complex displaying history of the Rappahannocks as well as other tribes. The Rappahannocks hold their annual heritage festival in August at George Washington's birthplace in Westmoreland County, Virginia.

UPPER MATTAPONI TRIBE
Mechanicsville, Virginia
Chief: Kenneth Adams
State Recognized February 25, 1983

The Upper Mattaponi Tribe is a group of urban, non-reservated Indians whose origin can be traced to both the Mattaponi and Pamunkey Reservations. The Upper Mattaponi are a people of high morals and strong ties to Christianity, and their community is centered around the Indian View Baptist Church. Adjacent to the church, the Upper Mattaponi built the Sharon Indian School in about 1919. The school was renovated in 1952 and closed in 1964. In 1985, the King William County Board of Supervisors agreed to return the school and two acres of land to the tribe. This structure is now used as a tribal center and meeting place for approximately 100 members. The Upper Mattaponi sponsor an annual spring festival to promote the culture and history of Indian people.

About the Authors:

Sandra F. Waugaman earned her BA from the University of Maryland. She began her career in Instructional Television at Richmond's PBS station, and then moved on to writing. In 1995 she started writing about Virginia Indian people and sites. Several of her articles and photographs won state and national awards. She won a National Press Women's award for a slide presentation she created based on the first edition of We're Still Here. She has also had two other non-fiction books published.

Danielle Moretti-Langholtz received her doctorate in anthropology from the University of Oklahoma. She is the director of the American Indian Resource Center at the College of William & Mary. In 2003 Governor Warner appointed her citizen-at-large to the Virginia Council on Indians.

On March 16, 2001, the Virginia Council on Indians presented their "Outstanding Citizen Award" to Waugaman and Moretti-Langholtz for their contributions to the advancement of the American Indian Culture through the book We're Still Here.

Index

Index

Index

Index

Share their stories!

To order additional copies of
We're Still Here
ISBN: 1-928662-01-3
[trade paperback]
Price $14.95

Visit: www.palaribooks.com
or write/fax/email

Palari Publishing
PO Box 9288, Richmond, VA 23227
Phone/fax: 866-570-6724
Email: orders@palaribooks.com

ORDER FORM:

No. of books _____ X $14.95 . . . . $ _____

Free Shipping . . . . $ – Free – _____

Virginia residents add 5% sales tax . . . . $ _____

Ship to:

Name _____

Address _____

City/State/Zip _____

Phone _____

Make check or money order payable to Palari Publishing.
Send to:

Palari Publishing
PO Box 9288, Richmond, VA 23227